Black Girl IRL

Life Between the Mess and the Magic

Gail Hamilton Azodo

Lawrence Hill Books

Chicago

Published by Lawrence Hill Books
An imprint of Chicago Review Press Incorporated
814 North Franklin Street
Chicago, Illinois 60610
ISBN 978-1-64160-929-6

Library of Congress Control Number: 2023949886

Cover design: Leah Jacobs-Gordon
Interior design: Jonathan Hahn

Printed in the United States of America

For the Black Girls, this one's for us.

Contents

Acknowledgments

Thank you to my family. My husband, my parents, my sister, my kids, our kids. Thank you to the friends that are family. To the girls' trips, to the late nights, to the endless chats. And thank you, Lord. For all the seasons, the beginnings and the endings. For always being right on time. Nothing in my life is without you. Win or lose, I am always thriving.

Introduction

You're an Everyday Black Girl

I want to start off bluntly: I'm not famous or influential. I'm actually the complete opposite. I follow more people on Instagram than I have followers. I routinely go out without makeup—so I'm by no means an "Instagram Baddie." My type 4c hair chronically remains untwisted and untamed in public, and the only people who call me regularly are my husband and my mom. How else do I know I am for sure a regular, noncelebrity Black girl? The other day I had to cancel a day of business meetings because I had urgent things to prioritize.

I needed to vacuum my house. That's what was urgent. Straight up.

I start off with this because I'm letting you know up front how real we are about to keep it in this book. This isn't some woe-is-me plea for pity, or a let's-feel-sorry-for-your-girl—because-she-can't-find-the-time-to-or-hire-someone-to-help-her-with-household-chores cry for help. This is just me, Gail Hamilton Azodo, canceling meetings to vacuum my house. Let that sink in. Some days I choose to watch this

1

machine whirl over my floors sucking up dust and debris instead of going to work because when everything else is going awry, this is the exhale, the release, the escape I need from sending one more "as stated below" or "as discussed" email.

As an adult, vacuuming, along with the myriad of other chores my Jamaican mother made me and my sister do before we were granted our daily ticket into childhood, has made the list of things I use to manage my stress and control my anxiety. So this satisfaction I now get from household tasks is either irony or a perfectly executed child-rearing plan.

And on that day, with my meetings canceled, my vacuum in one hand and my phone in the other, I was scrolling through my social media feed and feeling good. I was in the zone, concentration on point and my sense of accomplishment through the roof as I satisfyingly plowed through the dusty trail of Cheerios my one-year-old had left behind from his last snack time. All the while, I was mindlessly catching up on the lives of friends and strangers via social media. It was the middle of the day when I should be working—managing my business, replying all, or being productive in general—but here I was, vacuuming for leisure.

Before I could make it halfway through my living room, I was interrupted by a severe case of uncontrolled eye-rolling and a not-so-inner voice whisper-shouting "For real, though" and "Uh-uh, girl," brought on by what I was seeing on my feeds. It took about five minutes of this for me to actually realize I was no longer vacuuming but was instead solely engaged in my feed, trying to make sense of why my nonfa-mous, regular AF friends (please note: since everyone is a reflection of the people around them, I proudly accept my position as regular AF too, thank you very much) were all showcasing their basic lives with Hol-lywood filters and Black Girl Magic hashtags.

My immediate first thought was: Wait, did I miss Black Girl Magic day? I will NOT miss Black Girl Magic Day. Period. I already miss half of these made-up social media holidays since I usually check my feeds at night, and there are so many of these made-up holidays, I can barely keep up. I also always run into the possibility that my late-night post for "Favorite Sibling Day" will push up against the rush of overly ambitious early posters for "When Your Dog Was a Puppy Day" and make me look too yesterday. So, I usually just skip it all. But today, I was ready to participate. To confirm that it was in fact Black Girl Magic Day and that I did not miss it, I did a quick check of the celebrity social media feeds that I know would never miss a social media holiday, and quickly confirmed that it was a negative; it was not, in fact, Black Girl Magic Day.

Now it was time to investigate. Before you think too long—yes, I am that friend. Anything that doesn't make sense will become an in-ves-ti-ga-tion. Your new boyfriend's ex-girlfriend is still liking posts on his page? Investigation. New coworker moved here from the Midwest, attractive, no significant other, no kids, over thirty? Investigation. Everyone has that friend. You know her; she is me.

So I was now in full investigation mode. First rule of the investigation: Identify a pattern. What do all these over-the-top posts have in common? Get to work. *Scroll, scroll, scroll.* Boom, pattern found. Every single post was overfiltered and had a #BlackGirlMagic accompanied with an equally ambitious #Somethingsomethinggoals or #Somethingsomethinglife or #boss-something-type hashtag. It was like a formula had been distributed to every Black girl on my friend list and was on repeat all over my screen. At this point, I had to turn the vacuum off because I realized my loud inner voice was also fully engaged in an entire conversation:

Didn't So-'n'-So and I just talk yesterday about dude being the worst, and now you're dressed up with him like you're headed to the BET Awards #relationshipgoals #fitcouple?

Didn't you say that you hated your job because they didn't value Black women, and now you're in front of a computer with nothing on the screen and a fully beat face #lawyerlife #latenights #Getitdone #2amcrew?

Oh, and wait a minute, last time I checked, you said you were giving social media a break while you get your life in order, but now you're on here posting pictures from a trip I know you took last year #travelnoire #Blacktravelers #jetsetlife?

I was so distracted, I knew I would no longer be vacuuming for the day. I did, however, gather what I needed, and after reading all of these posts, I had so many questions.

———————

What I was seeing versus what I knew to be true in real life was perplexing, and it brought up some thoughts I'd been having for a while. Is this really the new norm for us Black women? We all know social media is a highlight reel full of happy moments and picture-perfect lives and rarely do we see realness. But I've been wondering, outside of social media, are Black women trying to live up to a 24/7 highlight reel? If so, where do we share our real experiences and learn from one another? Do we believe an unfiltered depiction of our lives would take away from the recognition we are finally receiving for our achievements, wins, and successes? Does the not-so-glamorous cancel out our magic?

This idea of every day and every moment being Black Girl Magic has become part of our daily lives—a validation of sorts. Events, birthday parties, and even conversations at times are either the one-up olympics or the *Amazing Race* to be Beyonce, and you know what? It's not always fun, friendly competition. It can get tiring. Don't get me wrong. I am the first one to throw a "can't outwork me" quote into the ether or add a "persistence and consistency is key" reminder to a conversation, but I also believe that there is equal value in celebrating and appreciating the normal, the repetitive, the average. As Black women, when did we stop valuing our everyday, nonglamorous lives and forget that our secret has long been in who we are and what we do naturally?

I grew up in a middle-class household that, outside of race and cultural nuances, could be any American household. I'm a child of immigrants, and my parents divorced when I was a teenager. I went to college and graduated. I wasn't the first person in my family to do so, nor did I have an athletic scholarship. My teens and twenties were great. Sure, I had my fair share of trysts and mischief, but they didn't involve me needing any rehabilitative programs or records to be expunged to make it through them. This doesn't take away from the good that can result from life experiences such as those, or those corrective initiatives, but that isn't my story, and it is also not the story of many of the Black women I know and who are my peers. Sure, there were and are periods of lows and the not-so-great stuff, as would be in anyone's life, but myself and many Black women are not overwhelmingly defined by trauma or traumatic events. We're just not. And I am the first to acknowledge that being able to have this experience is a privilege, or that I'm #BLESSED as we say on social media. Over a decade ago Nicki Minaj said it in her song "Moment 4 Life"—"No, I'm not lucky, I'm blessed, yes"—and to this day that still resonates with me heavy and I turn the volume up high when the song comes on. I also recognize that mainstream media and pop culture do little to show this normal life narrative or validate its existence, but it is one that many Black women are currently living. If I could summarize us, it would probably (not-so-eloquently) sound like this:

We are not famous, but we are for sure not

destitute. We are not stories of rags to riches and extreme strife, but we are also not permanently broken because we may have come from broken homes. Individually, we strive to do better than our parents, but we acknowledge that where our parents are in life isn't a terrible place either. In short, we are the Black women who make up the generation after the generation that watched their parents overcome, and we are thriving big time.

We were young in the 1990s, and LL Cool J called us the "around the way girl." We were a bit older in the 2000s when Kendrick Lamar appreciated us in "Humble." We are the unphotoshopped, something natural Lisa, Pamela, Renee Girl (those who know, know). Our daily lives may often be uneventful, but they are meaningful in their own way. They may not be doused with a heavy hand of Black Girl Magic, despite what the internet may tell us, but that doesn't mean collectively they aren't magical. In fact, they are more magical because, although often unseen, our day-to-day is impactful.

Growing up, I had an appreciation for the way my mom could do everything. Now that I am a mom and a patron of every Uber-Instacart-Shipt-Takl-Handy-like app possible, I still wonder how she was able to make dinner every night, have time for immigrant-style discipline, check homework, and pull off a full day of corporate America. It was a lot.

Personally, I tapped out of corporate America after ten years and started my own business, have a more fluid approach to childrearing based on each circumstance, and am still developing an opinion on the necessity of homework. What's true about both my mom's way of life and my current way of living is that they are both as normal as they are extraordinary. They both involve influencing the next generation, contributing to wealth creation, and connecting with loved ones. What's also true is that, by today's standard, neither would be worthy of a callout, a made-up social media holiday, or a celebration, and I think it's time we change that.

If you're reading this book, then you already understand what I'm talking about. You are or you have an appreciation for the real-life Black Girl, and this book is to support you and to support us. This is not an over-the-top call for validation, but a lighthearted, funny, and at times not-so-funny but always honest look at what it is to be a Black Girl in Real Life. No filter and no script. We are going to use this time to get into who we are because, whether people are watching or not, we are not just influential; we are instrumental.

If you ever doubt how profound our casual influence can be, I'll leave you with this story. A while back, one of my good friends, who is not Black, and I were heading out for a night at the club with friends to do things that girls in their late twenties with no real bills do, like drink, dance around in cute outfits, and eat McGriddles as a hangover cure when the night is over. This friend has always had the nicest professional-looking coiffed hair, like she just had a fresh silk wrap, so on this night, I decided to finally ask her what she does to keep this ongoing just-been-styled look. I assumed she must have been spending her time at one of these blow-dry-bar concepts that had become very popular among non-Black women. That's when she let me in on her secret. It turns out my girl was really my girl. She explained to me that in her freshman year in college, she had Black roommates and that she was always impressed with their Sunday wash day routine and weekday hair-wrapping at night, which always resulted in an effortless just-been-done look.

So my friend, after watching her Black roommates' routine enough times that year, decided to ask them to help her come up with her own routine so she could accomplish the same effortless daily look. She admitted that at first it was curiosity as to whether it would work on her hair type that made her ask, but surprisingly, it did. She came out of her freshman year of college with a life hack from the hair gods. She had a whole wash day routine that included a roller set, setting mousse, and nightly wrap. Ten years and counting, this was still her routine. As long as she wraps her hair at night before she goes to sleep, she can maintain that perfect hair look for the week.

Now I don't know how many people my friend has shared that story with or if, in the grand scheme of things, people's lives are changing because of it. In fact, I highly doubt these hair tricks will lead to world peace or affect climate change, but what I do know is that everyday Black women are influential, even when we are doing things that come naturally to us.

Like our roommate's Sunday wash day routine, we are the original life hacks. Our routines, styles, ideas, and overall being is influential. We are making our forever mark on someone daily.

This book is that affirmation that the everyday version of us, Black women, is enough. We are influential and important and, until now, there has not been a space where we can share our experiences. I've organized these experiences into a series of truths. Each truth is one I've personally been through and embraced as I daily step further into who I am—an ongoing process. My hope is that you too can relate to these truths, find your individual story within them, and feel even more connected to other Black women as so many of my girlfriends and I have by sharing our truths.

Most of all, this book is for us, by me, a fellow Black Girl IRL.

Truth #1

Silence Is Your Superpower

Black girls, are you feeling like how I'm feeling day in and day out? You know, exhausted?

For most people, there is a list of things that we spend our time and energy on; things like work, school, social life, family life, those are the norm. But in the life of a Black woman—a Black Girl in Real Life—there's a whole other list of things, responsibilities that we take on that the world has casually assumed is just for us. These range from serious "needs our most focused care and consideration" to really "why should this concern me, again?"

Things like: Providing our thoughts on race and injustice when every other week the news is detailing the offense on one or the other—serious. Being the primary defender and protector of all Black babies—serious now and for our future. Default contributor to the style direction and overall fashion sense for the masses—really? Can't y'all match colors? Is it really that hard? And oh, let's not forget the coveted title Black women carry as the original top chef before there was *Top Chef*.

The must-know-how-to-throw-down-in-the-kitchen. Couldn't that obligation be ended by just explaining to folks that salt and garlic powder are essential for *every* recipe? I said what I said.

Sometimes if I'm a bystander at work, or even out in these streets and hear people talking, or see something going down that needs to be resolved, I just know it won't be resolved until a Black woman steps in. I don't know where they are going to get her from or how she even gets there, but it happens. Out of nowhere, she appears. The original super-hero and fixer of all, the Black Woman. Maybe our genetic sequence is wired to have a mothering spirit that someone picked up on, because even during slavery, through hardship, we still had to mother everyone's babies, our Black babies as well as Their babies. Historians and sociologist have written plenty on the mothering Black women have been responsible for during that time but someone or some system has reinforced the idea to the world that Black women are a disproportionately respon-sible group and therefore we must now be respon-sible for *everything*. And it is exhausting. Is it an honor to have that high level of global trust, like a global security clearance of sorts, and be bestowed that level of responsibility? Maybe, sure. Is it also a burden at times? Absolutely, and it's *stressful*. What makes it even more stressful, exhausting, and unre-warding is that the number of times we are actually acknowledged, let alone thanked, for our nonstop save-the-world ability does not even come close to matching the number of situations we are called to spring into action for.

It's taken me years to juxtapose what seemed like an internal calling to be all things, to all people, all the time and the reality that no other gender and race combo has had the same generalized expectation to be the keeper of everything for everyone like the Black woman. None. We exit the womb as the matriarch. And because of that I often feel the ease of the lives of everyone else around me. There are the obvious times that I think many other Black women can draw upon, like in the workplace where it is clear my fear of failure, coupled with my need to overdeliver so that I can be taken seriously, is the exact opposite vibe of my white male counterparts. I was raised with the understanding that I would have to work twice as hard to get half as much, and yep, that's pretty much how things have played out in the workplace for me. But my nonminority peers? Their overall aura and demeanor appear to be calm, cool, and collected, which you know what? Good for them. I wouldn't wish this stress on anyone.

But then there's the unspoken but understood idea that Black women must always eat last, figuratively and literally. What do I mean? Think of every time you've been to any Black family's cookout or Thanksgiving dinner. Who puts together everyone's plates and makes sure everyone is fed and taken care of? Who is doing all the cleaning, table placements, and checking in to see if everyone has what they need? Who is doing this after they've planned, invited, prepped, cooked, put themselves together to look damn good, and welcomed and greeted the guests? Black women. I'm not saying that we can't or don't enjoy being of service to our people, but eating last at the table is just one spot on the long list of places where we are given the last slice. From salaries and job opportunities to family reunions and parties, Black women don't reflexively receive first dibs.

For me, having continuously experienced all of the above and then some—exhaustion and stress for just being who I am, a Black woman—I've finally reached the point in my life where if you have a question, need an opinion, want someone to chime in just for fun? Chances are it won't be me.

Silence is my new primary voice.

———————

It really started a few years back when I reached a breaking point. I was only a few months out from the opening of our latest venture, a restaurant, and a few months postpartum with my second child. People say never open a restaurant if you want to keep your money and sanity and I'm pretty sure they'd also say to never open one while you're pregnant with your second child and have a toddler going through the terrible twos. I was maxed out for a Black girl and for a middle-class human in general. If I saw just one more meeting invite come through on my phone, or one more random text, I wouldn't be able to take it anymore. I'd already experienced a panic attack before (more on that later) so I knew that the level of life recovery I needed at this point would require more than breathing in, holding my breath, and exhaling longer than I'd inhaled. I was over the breathing techniques. I'd not only done them all, Google was ready to *resume my search* should I feel like I may have missed one; I was beyond exhausted. I was mentally overwhelmed. I was fed up. I needed to get some sort of hold on my life and my day. I needed clarity, because sis could no longer be the be-all and end-all for everyone and everything. So I decided to evaluate my day-to-day obligations, like I've done before to no success. But I was suffering, so it was time to give it another go.

I thought to myself before *I'm not serious about life clarity and an organized schedule.* But post–panic attack, I was very much *Today, on this day, I'm all in.* This time I was going to get my life together. Fool me twice, right? I got my pen and paper and went to work. I was ready to get my life together in thirty minutes or less, bet. The name of the game: narrow in on what you really have to do. Not the long list of things you do but what are things that only *you* can do. No substitutions. No one else. Then everything else you either cancel or delegate, assuming you have the team and means to do so. With that, I was off to the races.

I began listing out everything I did on a typical day. Easy work. My day ranged: phone calls, kid drop-off and pick-up, laundry, meetings, errands, cooking, following up with clients; all of it made the list. The list was so long I had to take to the other side of the paper. It was lengthy; no task would be left behind. Next up, time to go through the list and cross out everything in red that I really didn't have to do, and it would be eliminated forever. I already knew this was going to be little-to-nothing on my list. Why would I be doing things that could be eliminated in the first place? Who stops making up their bed every morning? Where would those ten thousand pillows I don't even sleep on go if I didn't do it? And of course, I had to make sure my kids ate every day, and all the toys were picked up at night. And let's not forget inbox zero goals, so not check email, can't do that . . .

As predicted, there was nothing on my list crossed out.

Next up, time to highlight things I could delegate moving forward. OK cool, this will be my big opportunity area. There had to be some things here. *Remember So-'n'-So's birthday and send them a text.* Only I could do that; it wouldn't be personal otherwise. *Make dinner at least five days a week.* I mean, I could order out or get a meal plan, but that won't be the same, plus I don't know what those people put in their food. I don't want my kids eating fake food. My mom made every meal, every night of the week; I'm not trying to do less than she did. I'll just kind of highlight that one. I can figure something out for maybe one or two days of the week, if I really have to.

Last up, time to circle everything that only I could do and absolutely no one else could manage. I'm the Queen Bee in this house. These are the endless amount of things that make me special, right? Here comes my time to shine, or in reality, the lead up to my own demise.

I was already the doer of all the things, time to mindlessly prove it. And since I decided to get cute with this little thirty-minute exercise in tragedy, we already knew I was supposed to be crossing out and eliminating things in red because red means done, stop. Then I was half highlighting things in yellow for the soon-to-be delegated tasks I couldn't really give myself the permission to delegate, because yellow means proceed with caution, and I can't let just anyone take over my life. And for all the things that were *me, me, me*, you guessed it, I chose green. Sign my oldest son up for swim lesson, *me*. Remember to take the meat out of the freezer (which seems to be a common Black household problem from the beginning of time) so we have something to eat for dinner, *me*. Schedule team meeting to go over company goals, *me*. Call bank about fee charge on fee-free checking account, you guessed it, *me*. Because yes go, go, go! Go and get your life from all the naysayers that say you can't do everything. Keep control of everything, girl. This is your green light, a.k.a. go-ahead, to continue doing the most.

By the time I finished my little list exercise, my hands looked like I murdered a ninja turtle. I must have been unconsciously circling because almost everything was green. Nothing in my life could be eliminated, and as far as what could be delegated, I'd already bent the rules on myself and half highlighted items. In a "you can do it and so can I" spirit, I could cochair my life items. In my mind, my day was best executed only by me. I was the primary everything. One of one. I had to do it all.

I knew it made no sense. All the people I look up to talk about delegating and seeking help and here I am, unable to be helped. This couldn't be, and I didn't fully grasp it then, but I am here on the other side of all of that to tell you: that's not how it goes. You can't be the doer of everything and lead a life where you fully get to be you. You won't have the mental space to do so. Black women and, just as importantly, Black girls, you're not supposed to do it all and you shouldn't be handed the generational guilt that makes you think you have to, either. The world, our lists, are not our burden. We deserve a life and peace. The two can go hand in hand.

I'll also be clear here that just because I believe this, and hopefully soon you will too, doesn't mean it is easy. Since being on the other side of doing the most, I still fight against my overdoing it spirit, because it's deeply ingrained and against the expectations of others, which call for me to do more than what is required of everyone else. Now, however, if I don't feel inclined to, I just don't. And that's the pivotal difference in the mental state I live in today versus before. If I don't feel like it is overdoing it for the sake of overdoing it, and I feel inclined to go above and beyond, then I do. If it's just to prove my worth or assign an artificial value to my contribution to this world, then I don't.

Immediately after my green hands via list fiasco, I went into the breakdown I was so much trying to avoid. No panic attack this time, but I was frozen. I was in "I will not do" mode, to the max. I couldn't even begin to think about which green circle could become a yellow highlight, let alone a red strikethrough. My mind and body stopped. At that moment I did nothing, I said nothing. Well, let me asterisk that—I have two kids and a husband so "did nothing" is relative. It was more like I became a more restricted version of myself in regard to interactions and availability. I still had to pick up my kids from school in a few hours, make dinner and do bath time and bedtime routines, but mentally I was barely present. My inner control freak, type-A self was massively overwhelmed and had shut down.

How come other people were able to get their list and life in order and I couldn't? I was melting down from the swift defeat my list dealt me. My usual self, the first to respond to every text and call, just watched the phone ring and light up hour after hour as I let calls go to voicemail and left texts unread. If it didn't involve food or a bill to be paid, I was unavailable to the world. On day two, which was probably more like twelve to fifteen hours later, because in turmoil I tend to exaggerate and these feelings extend a minute into an hour, I abruptly got up and started responding to text messages from the emergency list of people who don't live in my house: my mom, my sister, my dad.

Apparently, what I thought was a dramatic reentry into their world wasn't even a thing. No one noticed I was gone. It's funny now, but at the height of my inner turmoil, it was shocking. I saw some texts between my sister and mom with links to new bathroom vanities my sister was looking at. Some comments on the latest *Real Housewives* episode, and then some goodnight texts. Apparently no one thought I was in danger. There were no "are you OK?" texts. It was a super-huge blow to my overdoing it spirit ego. I guess looking back, twelve hours wouldn't even be long enough to file a missing person's report, so it made sense. You can spend a lot of time making yourself be the be-all and end-all for things, perceiving that the world or the people in your world cannot function without you. The truth is they can and, even if it is difficult, they will.

———————

After that rude awakening, I decided to have lunch and placed my phone in front of me with the intention of checking my email. But the anxiety of even beginning to scroll through email after email was just too much. So I took a nap. Or rather the nap took me, because I woke up two hours later. Now I was ready. Awake with my phone in hand, I'd already planned out what my crisis control avoidance response was going to be.

> *Hi ___, so sorry I missed this! It's been so hectic, I'm just getting to my emails now. Please give me a call as soon as you get this.*

Let me go ahead and check to see how many things were now on the brink of demise in my life and what needed to be salvaged. I held my breath and opened my email inbox, double digit unread emails. It was a lot but not as terrible as I expected. I started from the top, where the newest messages were. Any emergencies would be there because, of course, the person would have emailed over and over again, trying to reach me. Five emails down and nothing yet. I was sure it was coming sooner or later. I reached halfway through the unread messages, made my replies—a combination of my preplanned crisis avoidance email template and just normal, non-time-sensitive stuff, and still no crazy red flag emergencies yet.

Again, ego bruised.

People were living their lives, and I was essential but not the be-all and end-all. This is not to say there couldn't be an odd chance an emergency could've happened during that time, but in my case, it didn't. Most things in my work life that are an "emergency" really were not. I don't work in any life-saving medical fields; I'm in hospitality. The shipment that we had to send out via UPS ground wasn't going to bring anyone back to life. If it were, it would be at least three to five days until it could.

The whole thing, from the list to my quiet demise to my uneventful reentry into communication, really put things into perspective for me. It was less about what I could do, or someone else could do, or even what I could delegate to someone else. It was about my energy. In my shutdown period, my conservation of energy was extreme, yes, and probably not a good model for having a healthy marriage and relationship with your kids, but I eventually stopped being frantic. At first, I was overwhelmed, but then I was calm after I got deep into not doing anything. I had voluntarily removed myself from texting, emailing, calling, and suddenly all of the constant communication felt like a sense of relief. Sure, my list was still there and needed to be addressed, because no, I still couldn't handle it all, but my entire being didn't feel stressed. I could start looking at things with a new nontense feeling. Dropping out of the world for that short twelve hours, in the extreme way I went about it, helped me find a calm I hadn't experienced before.

In a normal-but-not-so-normal way, we are all extremely plugged in at all times. Being plugged in means that you are essentially in communication, always. You are always relaying to the world what you like or don't like via social media, whether you are actually double tapping the like button or watching a video. You are telling someone something. Layer on being a Black woman and not only are we always telling someone something, we are always being asked and expected to say something, to communicate what we feel about something, and, very often, how we are going to fix something. I laugh when I hear someone say a Black woman needs to work on her communication skills. We are always in communication with the world, whether we like it or not. They must mean we need to work on how to deliver what we are communicating in a way that's easier for them to receive. Another item we need to move to the "thanks, but no thanks" pile. Being clear in what we decide to speak on and even more so what we decide not to speak on will have to be palatable enough.

With the taste that I got while being incommunicado, I was ready to try out this "say nothing" thing a little more, in the world and with my own people. Because there's nothing more exhausting than to be out in this world and then to come back to your space safe—your girlfriends, your family, whoever is part of your inner circle—and be back into everything-needs-a-response mode after just trying to catch your breath from it all.

I got schooled on the ultimate lesson of choosing silence for peace from my mother-in-law. One weekend, my husband and I were calling her so that we could check in on her and so the kids could say hello. We called her cell phone, her house phone—yes, she still has one—and even my father-in-law's cell phone, trying to get a hold of her. With every unanswered ring, it made the need to get an answer even more urgent. I don't know if it's just me but whenever I decide I'm going to call someone, like my aunt, mom, or older family member, if I don't get a hold of them, it starts to feel even more important for them to answer. Anytime they don't answer, the inner panic begins.

My mother-in-law eventually called us back, two days later. And when she did, it was in a tone as if she was returning our call from just minutes ago. "Hi, hello!" she said cheerfully. I was shook. Had she not seen all the missed calls? Of course she did.

I responded in my most impolite polite voice. "Didn't you get all of our calls?"

She replied, "Yes, that's why I'm calling you now. How are you guys?"

Wait, what? That's why you are calling us now, two whole days later?

"So what happened?" I pressed again.

"What happened to who?"

"To you guys? You didn't answer, and Dad didn't answer his phone either."

"Not every call is to be answered," she responded in a calm but blunt voice.

Again, wait what?

"Not every call is to be answered?" At this point I was thinking this must be some sort of trick.

"Yes, we have been resting, writing, doing some things around the house."

I was, once again, shook. No apology, no nothing. Didn't she know the type of panic that happens when we don't reach them? Call it my anxiety brought on by those 1990's Life Alert commercials but my mind instantly goes to an elderly person who has fallen and can't get up whenever one of our parents or older family members are unresponsive to our calls. I start thinking about if something harmful has happened. I start feeling guilty for not calling to check on them earlier, because who knows what might have been avoided if I called earlier than I actually did. So, after having gone through all of that personal guilt and worry, for my mother-in-law to respond so nonchalantly, I felt slighted. But I managed to pull it together and remain cordial.

"Oh, I see. OK, let us let you go. Glad you are doing OK."

"OK, we will talk again soon. Give the kids a hug from Grandma and Grandpa."

And then she hung up.

At this point I was still shocked by what seemed like a lack of regard for my time, my caring, and my consideration. I was so pissed, I called my mom immediately. I figured she would understand how unreasonably callous my mother-in-law had been. Nothing like the defense of your mom, right? Well, she did not understand. She couldn't understand why I would be so offended and so upset by someone who did call me back. Someone who was still alive and had other things to do than just sit and wait to answer every phone call that came through. Plainly said, someone who didn't feel the need to be tied to their cell phone, house phone, whatever phone minute after minute and had the freedom to take time to do things, everyday things, without feeling overly pressured to be in constant communication.

I listened to my mom. I understood what she was saying. But I was still pissed. I was pissed because she was right about my mother-in-law, and my mother-in-law had done nothing wrong. And because I wished I had that level of authority and discipline over my time when it came to respecting my own boundaries, to not feel the need to constantly be in communication. It was true: "Not every call needs to be answered."

We are always plugged in, always responding, and as Black women that's our reality times ten, and here I was being pissed at an older Black woman who rightfully has set boundaries around her peace. But even as I was thinking this, I was still pissed.

After I simmered down and stopped feeling some type of way, as I thought about it, I had an aha moment. My mother-in-law had cracked the code, and here she was ahead of me in where I wanted to be and recently aligned to when I had my life breakdown via organization list. The world of constant communication, even the type that comes from your family, at times can be quieted or, in this case, not answered. It is OK to not always be in communication or communicating, and I needed to be more OK with it for myself and others. I wasn't OK with it, even some time after my realization, but I am now. The whole ordeal with my mother-in-law gave me a new perspective.

Silence is how I recharge. It is my inner superpower.

Everything that I have experienced has always pointed back to silence actually giving me back my power. When the list activity "failed," the forced pause actually put me back in the game. It gave me the time to separate my fears from my thoughts, from reality, to determine what was truly necessary. When I dug deep inside, it was clear. *Not every call needs to be answered.* I still say it over and over to myself sometimes. *Not every call needs to be answered.* Silence is also an answer. A response to answer myself first. *Not every call needs to be answered.*

What are these "calls" in my life? I'll tell you what they are for me, and what they may be for you. By call I mean:

Text

Email

Question

Opportunity

Confrontation . . . yes, confrontation

All the things that present themselves as needing a response, and there are just so many that do. Have you ever considered that sometimes, the best thing to do about them is nothing? This is not about losing your job, or sacrificing your business, or being on the outs with your family because you don't respond to things you should respond to. This is about things you don't have to respond to, or don't have to respond to immediately, so you can protect your peace and your boundaries. So much about being a Black woman lies in our ability to solve things for others. To be there for others. To do things for others.

Choosing silence for me represents a shift we can take to pour into ourselves, solve things for ourselves. Whether that is working through a feeling, a plan, or the next big idea, there always seems to be a heightened sense of joy and giddiness I get when I take time to sit and think about the big things I can do and the things I will do. When my mind gets to reexplore everything I'm capable of, it feels really exciting. Being there for ourselves, because we deserve to show up for ourselves, whether we have something to do or not is important.

I recently went on vacation by myself and for myself. That was it, full stop. When anyone asked me what I was going to do, the answer was clear: nothing. We don't need to explain showing up for ourselves by just being present alone. Explanations are often left out when it's urgent that we contribute, right? It's often a rush, a tone, a sense of obligation that we move forward on. Well, I committed that time in silence from the world with that level of fervor and importance. It was a sense of obligation that I owed to myself, to be there for myself. I spent most of my time unplugged, writing, staring at my surroundings, and really feeling what it was like to be me. It was great.

There is an inexplicable peace in silence. When you accept that the world has to continue on, whether you participate or not, life gets clearer. Clearer about where and what your contribution should be. Clear about not answering calls that don't need to be answered.

For example, I have a homegirl, Ruth. Until recently, she was, to me, the most oblivious person in the world. Ruth never notices anything. When we used to work together, if I brought up how another coworker seemed snappy or their response felt rude, Ruth never seemed to pick up on the same thing. When we would hang out in social settings and I felt like someone was being loud or obnoxious or just plain too much, Ruth was never bothered.

It wasn't until years later when I was visiting DC where Ruth now lived and we were out catching up on life, telling stories about our old job and the city we used to live in, that I said to Ruth, "You never seemed to let anything about that place bother you."

Ruth laughed and said, "That's not true. I don't know those people; they aren't anything to me. So, their problems are their problems." She then went on to detail the "annoying characteristics," a.k.a. personalities and quirks, that she remembered about quite a few of the people we used to work with. She was spot on, detailing the same exact things that would be so bothersome to me years ago. This whole time, she knew what I was talking about! And one by one, she went through why it absolutely didn't matter for her day-to-day life.

Sure, they may have been bothersome or even borderline rude and aggressive to her, but the reality is only they had to go home to themselves and/or their family, not her. As Ruth put it, rather than respond to every verbal poke or slight, she continued on with the attitude that if they didn't contribute to her life beyond the workday, whatever they did or said was on them. I was floored. Ruth had heard and seen exactly what I was hearing and seeing all these years but never responded or commented or let it bother her? It was shocking and humbling. I instantly realized I talked too much. And that I was in deep need of that freedom. The freedom to allow people to be them, and me not having something to say about it every single time.

I immediately knew where I was going to test my new silence skill: my mom.

See, my mom and I have a very close relationship, thankfully, and I know that's a blessing. But as with any close relationship that also involves constant communication, sometimes every single thing becomes an item of scrutiny and response. And to be honest, it starts to create a strain in the relationship over time. It's a cyclical pattern. You're great for a while, then you're not-so-great, then you're back to being great. I wanted to get out of the cycle and normalize things. We deserved to spend less time in the not-so-great times. Besides, as we're both getting older, every not-so-great moment is like testing fate; life can change in an instant. This doesn't mean we won't ever disagree again but what it means is that, on my end, the degree to which the disagreement affects me would have to be minimized, and thus my responses will have to change. Because the reality is that my mom is a grown ass woman, and so am I. And although I respect her fully, she doesn't pay my bills nor is she critical to what allows me to exist day to day, now that I am an adult. I have a whole life in which no one is asking my mom to approve on my behalf, and she has lived a whole life, successfully I might add, without needing input from me on how to live it. The things that we may disagree on for the most part do not change my life and do not change hers. They also do not change the fact that we care about each other and love each other. My friend Ruth made me realize I needed to do better.

I immediately put my new "say nothing" plan into action, and I'm not going to lie, it was hard.

Me: "Mom, I'm thinking about cutting my hair"

Mom: "You always looked nice with long hair."

Do I look bad or something with short hair? I thought to myself. *At times it feels like I can never mention something without getting a contradictory response.*

Mom: "What did you guys have for dinner today?"

Me: "Just leftovers. I just got home, the traffic was terrible, and I'm tired."

Mom: "I used to drive two hours each way in traffic, pick you and your sister up after work, and make dinner."

That doesn't make me, right now, any less tired, I thought but still decided to say nothing.

Although in the beginning it felt painful inside at times, my outward responses were to say nothing or just politely respond, "Oh, OK." After a few weeks of what felt like deep inner turmoil from trying to gauge what really needed to be responded to and what could just be an "oh, OK," I was getting better. The burning urge to respond to everything receded significantly. After a few months, I became a pro—and what's even better, our relationship actually improved. My constant need to respond or have an answer was just doing too much. I saw how important it was to just let people be themselves, even in how they comment and react, when you have the opportunity to do so. My new vow of silence for the unnecessary was improving my relationship with the people that mattered to me most, not just my mom. The decreased conflict or feelings of being slighted gave me more peace and allowed me to do more, to think more, and to spend less time recovering from what I perceived as causing me emotional pain. With decreased conflict my joy was and has been increasing.

These acts of silence, whether they be in limiting my need to always respond, spending more time with myself unscheduled in the midst of a scheduled world, or even not answering a call or two have helped me increase my personal happiness. Voluntary silence has brought me joy. I have been quiet quitting conversations before quiet quitting was a thing. Choosing what I will and will not participate in has been the ultimate form of joy. I want all Black women to have this feeling. We deserve it. It is a necessity for Black women. Constantly being pulled in every direction, we need it for our survival. If we can get more joy without more being required from us, that is power. Black girls, Black women, we already know we can do it all; it has been historically bequeathed into our DNA. Spend time crafting your own version of silence, or whatever quieting you need to do in your life, so that you can harness more of your own superpowers and self.

Truth #2

Self-Care Isn't Selfish

You know what existed before mom guilt? Black girl trying to get some rest and take care of herself guilt. To this day I feel an immense amount of stress around taking time to take care of myself. Things like taking a five-minute mental health breather in the middle of the day or, God forbid, *a nap* sets off my nervous system and makes me feel like I'm about to commit a crime. Planning to take a whole day off? Or go on a trip by myself? Call the rest police because my Black girl self has to go through some serious mental gymnastics before I finally give into the thought that I actually deserve it.

There's something in us Black women that we have been conditioned to believe self-care and rest are things we need to be worthy of, things we need to earn. That the only way we can get rest is if we deserve it after some sort of difficulty or having accomplished something noteworthy. That self-care and rest is not built into our lives as a necessity but a reward that comes after and never during the phases of our lives. We also often experience guilt that, even after we reach the point in which we should receive the reward of self care, it still feels like we are not worthy. We hesitate to actually take the rest, to take care of ourselves and treat ourselves well. It's like we question the universe if it's sure this is for us. Like is it *sure* sure or is this just a set up? It has me thinking that the whole concept of self-care can feel unnatural for us, and it feels even more unnatural for us to actually do things that honor it.

Personally, I have experienced more guilt around treating myself well than anything else I've ever experienced guilt for in this life. Weekly, if not daily, I am presented with the opportunity to take care of myself, and every time the decision comes up, I grapple with it. As a Black woman, I know this to also be true for so many of us. From our beginnings, we've had to be a good daughter, a good friend, good student, good mentor, good leader, good activist, and maybe a good spouse or a good parent. Throughout all of those "good" roles, you know what we've also had to be? A "good Black girl."

Who knows what a "good Black girl" really is; there are so many nuances and societal pressures we feel when trying to fulfill every role in our life, and we're left feeling like we still haven't done enough. How do we show up where we excel in life and really hone in on that if we have to lend ourselves to doing some of everything? What I do know is that the good Black girl is overworked, overtired, and most important overdue for the rest and self-care she needs. To the good Black girl killing it in life and in relationships, or at least trying to, self-care can feel selfish. It can feel like a privilege. It can feel like if we are not actively doing for other people or playing the role of good [insert supportive role noun here], then we are taking time to ourselves that we should be giving to others, time we don't deserve. And it feels sad recognizing this.

I'm not sure when and how this no self-care life became our norm, Black girls, but I know I watched it play out in my family and in the lives of the Black women who surrounded me in my childhood. My mom, an aunt, a family friend—they all made sure everyone and everything else came first, with little time or energy left to take care of themselves. This behavior was ever-present and observed and, unfortunately, passed down generationally. It is however, doing us no good, Black girls. Abstaining from self-care and self-prioritization should not be our norm. Self-care is not only *not* selfish, it is necessary and essential for us Black women. It should be something we do daily. Self-care nourishes our inner Black Girl IRL selves; it lets us further enjoy this life we've put so much into. Self-care also is how you define it. It's what makes sense to you for how you honor taking care of yourself.

I can't stress enough how much the day-to-day action of self-care is important. It would be great to say we could just routinely hop on a plane and head to a one-week getaway at a secluded retreat to fulfill our self-care needs when they come up. And although that is all wonderful and I highly recommend you experience something like that at some point if you can, that doesn't solve for all the life moments in between. The need to honor ourselves on a day-to-day basis still exists.

We need to develop an individual self-care plan that assures our innermost self that we are worthy and supports us as we go through this life. It's the most unselfish thing we can do and is a way to express gratitude for who we are. It's what allows us to be soft with ourselves when the outside world presents so many opportunities in which we are dealt with in not-so-soft ways. Self-care is the softness, the gentleness, that we deserve and that we should get. Having a self-care routine is also how we let the outside world know that yes, we deserve it.

It is essential for us Black girls, and it should have always been.

Self-Care Is Time Alone

Who hasn't wanted to pack up and go on a solo vacation, relax, and not have to worry about a thing? Where your meals are taken care of, and rest is the agenda for the entire day? Oh, and all you have to decide is what type of restful activities you will partake in? Sign me up, sounds divine.

When I went on my first solo vacation that was not work related, I made no plans other than the plane ticket and where I was going to stay. I knew I would be fed and that I could do on a whim any relaxation-oriented activity I wanted to. That's all

I needed. Did I feel guilty? Of course. Did I think I was being judged? Yes, and to this day I still do. "What does a Black mother of two and wife think she is doing leaving her family for a week?" I imagined and still wonder if those comments were whispered about me during that time. But what I know is that time away felt great. I spent a week in mostly silence, ate, slept, and did nothing. I even got bored, and that felt great too. Apparently, I had forgotten what it felt like to be bored. The feeling of having absolutely nothing to do. Nothing to do other than to just let my mind wander freely and think about whatever it wanted to, new thoughts, old thoughts, or even the same repeated thoughts. In any other context I may have labeled this boredom as laziness, but because I'd intentionally had nothing scheduled, it felt completely appropriate. To have thoughts that weren't centered around what to do next or what plans I needed to make was freeing—and somewhat life changing.

I don't think I had fully remembered what my mind felt like at rest either. Do you know what your mind feels like at rest? And I mean, at *true* rest? Not planning, not doing, and not waiting for the next thing? I think Black women deserve to know this feeling, and to know it often. I feel like so many of us have never experienced that, or even fear experiencing it. Fear that if we are not always in doing or planning mode, it's an indication that something must be going wrong in our lives. What my solo vacation gifted me is the realization that just like silence, time alone is important. And that the foundation of my personal self-care routine is time alone.

Time alone is achievable for me daily and for you too. You don't need a plane ticket or secluded hotel stay to get there. Of course, an entire week alone is always a great way to achieve solitude but you can get to that place even if a few minutes a day is all you have. I know variations of how I achieve my daily time alone can be called mindfulness or meditation, and it may turn out to be one of those things for you. Whatever you ultimately call it is fine, the most important thing is that you take it.

There's a perception that, given the big lives that we Black Girls lead, we need equally big time away to reset or decompress. That anything less than an epic exit or pause from our day to day just doesn't count. Sometimes a few minutes of pause is all we need, and here's how I do it. When I'm in the middle of a hectic day or what feels like ten thousand never-ending things that make an escape feel like the only way I can mentally feel clear, I just stop. I sit at my desk, put my phone on do not disturb, close my lap-top, then set a five-minute timer. I take the time to just breathe and let any thoughts flow or not flow. I am alone with my thoughts and myself in that moment. Everything else may be continuing to swirl and, to be honest, sometimes it feels like I'm wasting the little time I have. But on the other side of it, I always end up feeling more in control of my day and my thoughts.

I feel more centered.

Technically, there's no one way to get the time alone that you need, and it's important for you to take the mental reset that you need and deserve. But given the already overcommitted and overscheduled lives we live, time alone does not always have to look like removing yourself from the people around you or your day-to-day life. You don't need to quit something to be observant of getting time alone on the regular. Plus, Black women don't need another thing to plan for in the already limited time we have to give ourselves. While it's fun and important to look forward to and maintain scheduled times in which your whole Black girl self—mind, soul, and body—is on a retreat from your obligations, you can in the meantime take the mental retreat available to you right now by taking that moment or moments during the day to stop and pause, to let your thoughts flow. So take time to consciously mute the outside world for a few minutes and create a mental space in which you are alone with your thoughts, time alone to think and to process and to even get bored while the things in our lives continue to move at lightning speed. For me mental pause is one of the most underrated self-care hacks. It's available to us all and truly beneficial to the type of lives we live as Black women. We don't have to wait weeks, months, or even years to get a mental break.

We can give ourselves one right now.

We often take for granted our ability as Black women to be constantly doing. It feels so natural to us, we don't really recognize that our minds are constantly working without rest. It's a sense of accomplishment for us to show up and do the most. But taking a break? There's often no one making sure we get that done. And if there is someone like that in your life, don't ignore them. It's *good* advice. And if you don't have someone in your life constantly telling you to take a break, let me be that person for you.

I'm always going to advocate and root for my fellow Black girls to be their best; I, for one, want to change the narrative around our success and rest, and I want us to recognize that mental self-care, rest, and success all go together. We can do our part with affirmative words like, "Congratulations, sis! Have you taken a moment to yourself to reflect on your awesomeness?" and, "I'm so proud of you and everything you've done. I hope you get time to take it all in." These are great examples of how to support a Black girl while making space for her rest. Our big moments, in our big lives, sometimes just need little pauses. We can and should create our own systems to incorporate the time alone we need and to become stewards of encouraging our community of Black women to do the same.

Self-Care Is Asking for Help

I used to be notorious for sending a request or asking for help with something and then just doing it myself. I would also then talk about all the things I did and got no help for. These were highly contradictory actions, and I knew it, but my Black-girl-doing-the-most wiring at times just wouldn't let up. If anything, I've learned and observed that we Black women can be hesitant to ask for help. I'm not just talking about domestic help, although that is helpful to get. I'm talking about help in all the different areas of our lives. The help that will let us go farther faster, without having to assume all the responsibility ourselves. The help that we may think labels us as lazy, unintelligent, or weak. But does it really? Or is this just an assumption we have made because we have never seen asking for help modeled for us in the past?

There's an African proverb originally from Burkina Faso that says, "If you want to go fast, go alone, if you want to go far, go together." If our ancestors knew this to be true, when did we Black women begin abandoning the notion of help being a necessity? I say it so many times not only because it is true, but because it deserves to be said repeatedly. It is a truth that isn't recognized often enough: Black women are solely and unequally responsible for so much, and for the most part our responsibilities are not met with assistance. We influence lives, break career barriers, and lead families all without help. One of the biggest things we can do to take care of ourselves as we continue to bear all of those responsibilities is to ask for help. And not just ask for help, but also actively identify what parts of all those responsibilities that we have we can delegate and get the help we need and deserve.

There are no trophies handed out for Doing Everything, Always. The only award for this is the inevitable burnout and emotional exhaustion that comes with trying to carry everything and everyone on your back. So, sis, I say this with all the love and affection I have for you and us as Black women: even if you're resistant to the idea and your pride feels a little bit (or heck, a lot a bit) bruised, please ask for help anyway.

Ask for help and accept it when it appears. Even if you feel some kind of way before and after accepting, keep practicing asking for help as a skill and an essential pillar of your self-care routine. Getting comfortable with asking for help comes from doing it over and over until it becomes second nature. And while I'm no psychologist, we don't want your Doing Everything, Always to become a form of self-harm, a way to punish yourself unjustly and cruelly for an inaccurate and perceived failing you think you may or may not have. So I'm here to tell you, no, you're not failing by admitting you can't do it all. You're admitting that you are human—we are *all* human—and your humanity needs rest, just like we all do.

We also need to get away from the kernels of fear that sometimes hide within Doing Everything, Always. Fear of your household falling apart. Fear of losing your job. Fear of being seen as a bad friend, daughter, mother, sister, coworker, activist, businesswoman, caretaker, visionary, thinker, doer, dreamer, writer, planner, etc. So I must ask another, potentially feather-ruffling question: What is the worst thing that could or would happen if you took care of yourself? What is the worst thing that could or would happen if you paused for five minutes, ten minutes, an hour to breathe through your stress, and recenter yourself? What is the worst thing that could or would happen if you got back to doin' you, just for a little while, so you can feel that spark of joy and zest for being here on this earth and not tired all the time? What would you do if you weren't afraid?

I hope that answer is rest.

Self-care is not only what you do for yourself, but also what other people do for you so that in turn you can do more for yourself. When I said I was known for asking for help but then doing it myself, that is the exact wiring and mindset we all need to let go of. But I know that it is a trait that is oh so familiar to us Black girls. Remember that time to take a pause? How much more attainable does that become when you are actually letting people help you? There are things we are meant to do and be, and those things we as Black women will always contribute our unique abilities and expertise to so that it gets done. And then there is everything else that is not proprietary to our Black Girl Magic that we can get help doing.

The biggest barrier to accepting that asking for help is a necessity for self-care is the perception that being helped is a form of weakness or laziness. How are companies run or even countries? With teams of people. If it's not a weakness to need people, plural, to run global economies, then Black girls, it can't be a weakness to need other people as you lead the running of your life. When I see my mom, to this day, work a full schedule, cook, clean, cater to every family

member, and show up to every event its impressive—
but it's also exhausting. I don't remember my mom
ever asking for help. Even as my sister and I have
gotten older, she is still hesitant to ask us to assist her
with anything. Mother's Day dinner for ten, that's all
her, no help needed or wanted.

I am actively working for that to not be me, and I
hope that you are too. Not because we can't do it and
won't do it if it's necessary, but because it's not always
necessary and doing everything should no longer be
a badge of honor to prove that we are not weak or
lazy. We already know that Black women are not lazy,
our history credentials us as relentlessly hardworking
and overworked. Those credentials more than carry
us into the future. Our time to ask for and get help is
now. We don't have to outdo ourselves any further to
prove our worth.

If I ever thought a group of people were poised to
take over the world, it is Black women, and I just want
us to be around to be able to do it. We need to ask
for help so that we can keep on doing the work that
we are doing. Starting with our personal and familial
lives, are there things we don't have to be responsible for all the time? I can't tell you what that looks
like for you, but for me it's simple things, whether
it be shopping for groceries, cleaning up, or making
the decision of where we are going out to eat. Not
being the one always doing those things or making
those decisions frees me up time-wise and mentally
to enjoy being with the people that I care about the
most. Have you considered what you cannot do and

instead turn over to the help of others so that you can enjoy more of your time here on earth with friends and loved ones?

When it comes to my work and career, I always have big ideas and plans and, in the past, I have always tried to be the one who executes all those big ideas and plans by myself. And while I often passed off my inability to delegate as being the one who could do everything the best, the truth was me not being able to ask for help and being ashamed to ask for help was killing me. Not being able to ask for help is not only mentally stressful, but it also can take a physical toll on you.

My inability to seek out help to reach my goals was rooted in shame and a lack of trust. Not trusting that they would execute to the standards that I would or that they would be committed to it as well. But also fear of being judged and labeled as lazy. But you know what? As I began asking for help more and more, it got easier. Me asking for help, especially in the areas where I was not the subject matter expert, not only helped me reach my goals but also helped other people reach theirs. Some people's goals align to them being the best in areas that help you reach your goal. If you keep the focus on your goal, delegating to a team can get you there and then some. How much of a disservice have you been doing to yourself by not seeking help in the professional setting? Can your days have more focus and rest if you're not doing everything? None of this is new news and none of it is meant to be. I'm just reintroducing what our ancestors knew so that we can begin to reprogram what generations of hard work has led us to: a life in which in asking for help feels like the opposite of Black Girl Magic. When in reality there is no shame or weakness in going farther by going together and having help in our lives.

Self-Care Is Sleep

Sleep may be the biggest game changer of self-care. Why? Because sleep is the manifestation of rest in physical form. Sleep is repeatedly touted as the first step in one taking care of themselves in terms of health and is a vital factor for longevity. When sorting for race and gender, a Yale School of Medicine study published in the *Journal of the American Medical Association* found that Black women had the short- est duration of sleep due to several societal reasons.[*] This should come as no surprise to us. Societal rea- sons for reduced and diminished sleep quality range from discrimination to economic and familial factors. Black women are the glue of our families, are con- stantly breaking down economic barriers, and are the collective mothers of the painful racial violence that discrimination leads to. Sleep—good sleep—more than likely doesn't come easy for most of us. Even more so, being tired or busy (which is just another way of saying tired these days, let's be real) is often

---

[*]César Caraballo et al., "Evaluation of Temporal Trends in Racial and Ethnic Disparities in Sleep Duration Among US Adults, 2004–2018," JAMA (April 7, 2022), doi:10.1001/jamanetworkopen.2022.6385.

expressed as a badge of pride, like evidence that we are indeed checking every box.

I, for one, am less concerned about manifesting a tired life as proof that I'm actually doing things in my life. I want to be successful and rested. I don't think it has to be either/or. You can have all the magic, Black girls, and get some sleep. Surely there are times in our lives, like when you are starting a new venture, having young children, or experiencing sorrowful moments, when sleep naturally escapes us all. This is understandable. But to continually push ourselves to points of no actual rest because anything less means you are not worthy of the life you've built is a mind set we have to get out of, sis. Not to belabor a point, but I've found the best way to ensure that I get some sleep is by asking for help so that I have time to sleep. When I'm not being the one woman show, I'm naturally more rested.

Sleep, however, is not a reward. I need to say that one more time, *sleep is not a reward*. In fact, sleep is how we are able to continue to exist. What machine runs nonstop? Even a computer needs to be rebooted and updated. Surely, you value yourself, your mind, and your body more than your Macbook. Furthermore, you are not the world's first forever non-rebootable machine. Sleep, as basic as it may sound, is how you will fuel and refuel your biggest and boldest manifestations. That is not possible with the lack of sleep.

Also, when did it become taboo to take a nap? Naps have always belonged to infants and toddlers.

In that age group naps are generally longer than what an active adult has time for, lasting hours at a time. Caretakers are, though, consistently met with a more tolerant child on the other side of them, ready to take on the next part of their day with less incidents. Naps *change* things. Naps for adults, on the other hand, receive the mark of laziness in some people's eyes. Try telling a Black mom you're an adult about to take a midday nap, and you'd think you said you've decided to quit life. I can't count how many times my mention of needing to take a nap was met by a "Must be nice" type comment from my mom. But understanding that Black women have been expected to work nonstop I understand her reaction. It's in her programming.

But naps are OK, Black girls! If anything, they are more than OK. Research shows although you don't need to nap if you're a healthy adult, taking a nap can have many positive benefits.* Short naps can improve your alertness and performance. Hit a mental block and taking a few minutes to clear your thoughts is still not giving you what you need? Try taking a nap. A nap doesn't have to be hours, nor does it have to be daily. This is not a new task for you to focus on, schedule, or accomplish, since I know how we overachieving Black girls can be. This is about giving yourself permission to take a nap if you have the time to do so and to do so peacefully, setting self-judgment aside.

While lying down and taking a nap will remain a

---

*"The Benefits of Napping," National Sleep Foundation, May 10, 2021, https://www.thensf.org/the-benefits-of-napping.

novel idea for many of us, I don't want to understate how important getting good sleep is for us. Black women don't need to continue to battle everything plus the consequences of not attending to one of our body's most basic needs, sleep. Before I even work on lengthening something that may be beneficial for me, like sleep, I work on improving it. Quality over quantity. Because as we know, realistically, we may not be in a life stage where more sleep is available to us. It just is what it is. But improving the sleep we are getting? Yes, we can absolutely do that.

And to do that, let's build on the idea of sleep being self-care and create a routine around it. Having a sleep routine puts emphasis and importance on sleep. We've decided not only to prioritize our sleep, but also to let other people in our lives know that this is our time. Here are some things you can consider as you build out your individual routine: a consistent time, lighting, ambient sounds, and what you do immediately before you sleep.

Having a consistent time when you go to sleep, tells your body *this is the time I rest*. This is the time that belongs to me. Along with time of day, another signal to our bodies that it is time to rest is lighting, or in this case the lack thereof. Darkness is tied to our circadian system; light in general during sleep reduces our sleepiness and ability to have rested sleep.* We were built to awaken as dark shifts to

---

*Christine Blume et al., "Effects of Light on Human Circadian Rhyths, Sleep, and Mood," *Somnologie* (August 20, 2019), doi: 10.1007/s11818-019-00215-x.

light, therefore any constant intrusion of light can affect your overall sleep quality. And while keeping a dark space is important, the type of lights you see before bed are equally important. Smartphones, computers, tablets, I love them all but leading up to sleep they don't love you. The constant blue screen exposure can delay your circadian clock and sleep. Keeping them in the same room and having them flash notifications while you sleep? Also not helpful for getting good sleep. Lastly, sound, ambient noise, or low frequency background noise helps drown out other sounds and promote rest and relaxation. It's why some people sleep best on a rainy night or with the engine murmur of a plane on a long flight.

Sleep, and sleep as self-care, begins long before you actually need to sleep or take a nap for that matter. It starts with you giving yourself guiltless permission to get the sleep you need in the quantities you need it and at the times you want to. There is nothing heroic or that makes you more deserving of your Black Girl Magic in forgoing your innate need for sleep and rest.

Black girls, in this version of our real lives, as we influence the next generation, I want us to get some sleep like what we deserve.

Self-Care Is Unapologetic

In the background of everything that self-care is and can be is the fact that self-care is unapologetically about you and what you want and what you need. It is ownership and acceptance of the decisions you make that are best for you, because you decided they are best. The decisions don't require sign off or acceptance by anyone else. They reflect your best interests because only you would intimately know your own best interests. Black girls, as paradoxical as it may sound, for self-care to not be selfish you've got to put others aside and choose you. Black women are nurturers and problem solvers. We not only always seek the solution, but at times we *are* the solution. Doing for yourself means setting aside the desire to always nurture others and prioritize nurturing ourselves. So how do we show up unapologetically in a way that demonstrates self-care?

Leading with your true self.

For example, for years in my twenties and thirties I felt the pressure from people questioning why I wasn't married yet or why I hadn't settled down. Every year as I got older it seemed like new people joined the chorus of "Where is your husband?" It was as if these people were sad for me, when I didn't feel sad at all. I felt overwhelmed by their concern at times. That is, until I came to the realization that after lots of bad dating experiences (more on that later), for me being unmarried and unwilling to settle just to settle was the best thing I could do for myself. It also would have been massively unfair to the person I married, because I wouldn't be showing up to our entire relationship as my full self if I didn't want to be there in it in first place.

You see what I'm saying?

It was a bold thought for me to have and live by, but it represented my truest feelings and my best self at the time. Being unmarried was my form self-care during that period. By choosing me, I was allowing whatever other person to find the right person for them and spare them the festering resentment of "this is not who I married." Because we all know that couldn't last long. The process of uncovering a completely different version of yourself is not only personally revealing but could be detrimentally revealing to a relationship or marriage. It would have been selfish of me to not do the work to uncover who I really was and commit an inaccurate version of myself to my future partner.

Having the space to understand and be my authentic self without also having to show up for someone else was just what I needed. For a Black woman to decide when and if she wants partnership doesn't say anything about her other than she's made a decision that best reflects what she wants, point blank. It is easy to be guilted into the life other people think you should live and the timeline they think you should have. The same pressure that other people were putting on me about when I would get married was also pushed around my decision to have children. Having or not having children is no one's decision but your own. Wonderful lives are had with and without children.

For a Black woman to be open about what she does and does not want is often shocking. Decisions around not wanting marriage, not wanting children, or not wanting to be in a relationship that is no longer serving us—most of us Black girls have few examples of how we should navigate these choices, and we definitely aren't openly encouraged to say no to these things. Because of that it can be more difficult for us to step up and embrace who we don't want to be, even though that's the clearer decision.

And decisions about marriage and children are only the tip of the iceberg. Choosing yourself can be about going back to school or even going in the first place, or starting a business, moving to a new place, changing jobs, staying friends with someone (more on that later, too, because whoo girl . . . that one's tough), and a plethora of other things. Either way, saying no to who you are is not self-care. Rejecting who you are not *is*. We do not have to passively accept a life that is expected of us if that's not what we want. Unapologetic self-care is about showing up for and choosing yourself time and time again, and rejecting all the things that you don't want to do or that don't serve you just as definitively as you choose the things that you do want to do and the things that give you life.

It's also choosing the people you do and don't want in your life, which leads me to our next truth.

Truth #3

(Successful) Dating Is Just Simple Math

I'm going to start this off by saying that when it comes to dating, I'm not the expert. I'm just the observer. That's not to discredit what I'm about to go into but to provide useful context to you. It's also to further credential myself (yes, I said credential myself). An observer with advice, that's basically what a coach is. Some of the greatest successes in sports have been accomplished with the helpful guidance from observers with advice, that is, coaches. Think *Iyanla, Fix My Life* meets Oprah's *Super Soul Sunday*. Consider me a life coach because dating is pretty much a sport these days. A coach may or may not have had significant time as a player in the game themselves, but they all have the skillful observer's eye to critique and provide valuable feedback to the players so that they can play the best and essentially win.

I'm here to offer real Black girl dating coaching so that you can win—and by win, I mean date to find the partner that's right for you. If you're already boo'd up, that's OK. You can come along for the ride or even coach from the sidelines; we're all in this together.

One of the biggest issues I experienced while dating was the "How the hell did I get into this mess?" feeling I'd get immediately after a relationship or "situationship" was over. Like how come so many weeks, months, or—God bless my previously naive soul because I used to think time was endless—*years* have gone by and I'm just now realizing this was just a setup to waste my time that has been disguising itself as a relationship. I met my exes at work, the club, through friends, in social groups—you name it. Everywhere except church (too late for that one, now that I'm married), but based on my previous pattern of dating, where and how I met them wouldn't matter. It was all a mess.

My decision-making process was just flawed. Correction, the *lack* of a decision-making process was what was flawed. That's right, there was none. Well, none that were tied to what long-term success with a partner should look like. Looking back at it, my dating technique probably looked more like a game of spin the bottle. There were no real similarities between any of the ex-partners who were just randomly sucked into doing things together for extended periods of time that basically became my relationships. Yeah, sure, there were conversations about "becoming official" or the slip into official where we were doing things together long enough that being "official" was just assumed. I now see that these were mostly relationships of convenience, or me just wanting to be in a relationship just to be in one, not relationships based on what I deserved or, for that matter, what my former partners deserved.

Eventually, a pattern emerged for me. After each failed relationship, it was easier to get into the next one or even a serious "talking" situation as if the next relationship would be the fix for the last. Motivated with goals and you have a career? Perfect, that can make up for my last relationship where there were no long-term life plans and jobs changed every quarter. I'll just disregard the lack of commitment and unavailability at certain times of the night.

Sound familiar?

I am going to interrupt myself here and say that I'm the first to admit that not all dating has to be for the serious intentions I'm about to go into. Not all dating is for marriage. I personally didn't start dating for marriage or long-term couplehood until I was in my late twenties. There was a life to be had. By the time I got married, I had friends who had been married for ten, even fifteen years. I was not ready to be married at the age they were, and that was OK. I was happy for their marriages—and happy for my lack of seeking one during that time. So, if you're not ready to settle down, do you, boo. No explanation needed. It's OK to date just to date, no strings attached, if that's your full intention. As it is said, clear is kind. It's better to be up front about wanting to date just to date than to lead someone on. However, when you are ready to find your someone of someone's, your life partner, your love of a lifetime . . . you get the gist, come on back here and pick right back up where you left us!

Now, back to what I was saying before. The relationships I was in were not what I really wanted at all; these people definitely could not be my life partners. None of them. No ma'am, I refused to believe the Lord would set me up like this. They were the exact opposite of "won't He do it." For me, I just know He did not! The question to myself, though, was "What am I getting so wrong?" These cannot be the only fish in the sea. I need a new ocean!

After years (yes, I said years) of successfully getting it wrong, I finally got it right. It took a little realignment and *cough* humbling of myself *cough* but when I got it, I got it and I felt *good*. Eyes wide open, with a plan and a commitment to put in the work for dating, I succeeded. I am and have been with the person who is My Person. The one for me, the one that I feel like I can be my whole, complete self with. There's no version of me he hasn't seen or is waiting to see. In my opinion, there's no better feeling than knowing that there's someone who has my back, supports my dreams, and is invested in me as a person, day in and day out.

In childhood that person may be your parent. But when someone takes on the role in your life by choice and with love, romantic love, it's a special sort of magic. It's not rosy all the time. We aren't in suspended bliss with no conflict or differences. But that's the best part of finding your person—that conflict and those differences don't change your connection and your commitment. For me and my partner, we chose each other and continue to do so over and over because we both made a conscious decision that had some clear and key requirements, one would say. How did I get to this point after living through what seemed like it would be the never-ending dating saga? Well, it all started with BAD MATH.

I definitely know how to add and subtract. I can do basic math pretty quickly in my head in most scenarios. Long numbers with decimal points, though, you may see me using my finger as I write it out on the invisible chalkboard. Same with multiplication. I'm good with the basics; get into the double digits, the air chalkboard might make an appearance. And division? Well, I have an iPhone. My math skills are appropriate for my age. I'm past the age where someone will quiz me on long division or addition of double digits, let alone multiplication of double digits, so I consider myself pretty proficient. I can get around in life, manage my budget, and I have a general idea of how much my bill will be when I go shopping at the store. (Except when the store is Target; those numbers there never add up. But that's a different story unto itself.)

Math is one of the most essential skills needed through all walks of life. Get the basics down and you're pretty much set. The complicated stuff? Good to know how to do it for your ninth grade AP exam, but no need to do it on your own since the completion of your high school graduation and the invention of the smartphone. Your own portable TI-84. But while math just finds its way into all facets of our lives, who would have thought that *dating* would become a part of my life that needed some categorization with the help of numbers? That the real reason I was getting everything messed up was really, really bad math? And that I had the tools to fix it just by making a little shift in my thinking and my intentions?

It. has. been. life. changing.

I'm going to get into it, but first let me give you the part you need to remember and that makes everything about what I'm going to say really simple. You know how in an algebraic equation, what's on either side of the equal sign must be the same number? Like 4+5=7+2, or 5×10=25×2. And how what you do to one side, you must do to the other, so that it stays equal? Well, that's the not-so-secret secret to all this: you must keep the equation balanced. That's the good math. One side, which is you, must equal the other side, which is them. That's it, that's all there is to it. Now let me get into it so you can start building your own relationship equation.

Often as regular Black girls, Black girls IRL, we are doing our thing. Our careers, we've got that on lock and are making strides. We are moving up the corporate ladder, or we are business owners, or we are lifestyle influencers, or all of the above. Our social lives, they are finally at that point where we are comfortable with who we know and who we don't know. We are leaning in close to the ones that need us and that we need. Our tribe is our people. In our family life, there are some ups with some downs, but who doesn't have that? We know where we come from and we know what generational traits to take with us, and which ones we are leaving behind, because generational curses end with us. And last but not least, our dating life? Meh, it's there.

Our dating life success is not matching up with dating successes. "The One" has turned into "Not the One" a few more times than we would like, and at this point who knows what "The (Actual) One" really looks like anymore. Even perfect in-person and on paper can turn into the next "it would be perfect if they ended it first" or "are people still ghosting each other?" We spend so much time checking off life goals; everything seems to be going at the right pace. But as soon as we get to the "love of my life" box, the check mark isn't there, has faded, or life has just shown up with a dirty eraser and slowly smudged it away.

To feel like you have a whole life and are a whole person but are navigating it without a life partner can suck. And actually, if that is something you really want in life, then it does suck. We shouldn't be afraid to say that. This isn't about waiting for someone else to come along and complete you and make your life meaningful, 'cause, no sis, we are not about that life. We seek to be complete people first and foremost. We are cozy with ourselves. Then, when we have committed to doing the work and to keep doing the work, we look for the same. I did not start on the process of finding "The One" under my new terms until I felt like the work I was doing on myself was at a place that I could transparently share with a future partner where I was at and what I was seeking, flaws and all. I also say this, and most people are taken aback by it, but really when I went on my journey to finding my future life partner, I also was comfortable enough to know that journey may just direct me back to myself. I had a sense of peace that if I did not get married or committed to a single person for my entire life, that in itself was OK.

I thought about the elements of marriage or partnership I wanted and then each one of them I laid out what would be the plan if I had to fulfill them myself. If the divine plan was not to, say, have a partner I had children with, I was OK. For me that one was easy since I knew that even within a partnership the ability to conceive wasn't a given. I knew, though, that whether I wanted biological children or was open to adoption, science and a multitude of resources were there, and I was confident I would pursue mothering with or without a partner. For other things, I had to dig deep and seek a solution that was me-focused. Things like the desire to have date nights and someone to be a confidante. When I thought about it, nothing technically stopped me then, or even now, from taking myself on date nights. I used to be so self-conscious about going out and doing things alone. So I forced myself to do it, to go to all the restaurants I was waiting to go to with the right person, or the events at which I feared people would stare at me since I wasn't there with someone. And I survived! Everything was OK.

I'm not saying that my lifelong solution for if I ended up not having a date night partner would be solo adventures. What I am saying is that I wasn't open to the idea that companionship doesn't always look like a romantic partner, and I would have been stuck not living my life, waiting for "The One." Yes, I had myself first and foremost, but I also had other relationships in my life. Nonromantic ones, but loved ones, friends and family that I enjoyed doing things with and vice versa. So why not invest in those relationships as well and continue to add the experiences I enjoyed to them. I actually enjoyed going to a great dinner with friends just as much as a date.

I continued on with my list of all the things I thought would be "missing" if I never found my life partner, and by the time I was done evaluating whether they really would be missing, I felt comfortable with where I was at mentally. Life could and would be lived regardless of the outcome from the intentional and calculated dating adventure I was about to embark on. I recommend you think through those things too, the things that, if you had to move forward on as yourself, unpartnered for the rest of your days, may feel scary. How would you eliminate that fear and start fully living now?

As I revealed before, the key to my dating self-intervention was to keep the equation balanced, to practice good math instead of bad. To make sure one side equaled the other, and what was done to one side of the equation was also done to the other side. My balanced dating philosophy I called the "Black Girl

IRL Partner Rating System" or "BGIRLPRS." Super long acronym, but stay with me. BGIRLPRS is based on both tradition and observation.

BGIRLPRS starts and ends with being equally yoked. I used to hear my mom say that phrase all the time: "You must be equally yoked." She applied this to friends, family, and relationships. It was the reason some relationships had successes and others had failures, in her opinion. If you grew up going to a Black church or being around older Black folks, you probably heard it a lot too. That's one thing about our people, they can throw an "equally yoked" statement into everything. I've seen it written so many ways too, including "equally yolked" like the yolk from the center of eggs. In the Bible, it comes from 2 Corinthians 6:14 and refers to being unequally yoked or joined with nonbelievers. The yoke is what joins two oxen via their neck. And when two oxen are yoked, that is, joined together at the neck, they need to be equal in size, stature, and ability so that they can work together effectively. Thus, equally yoked.

Listen, I'm going to be transparent here. Dating as I understand it in any year post 2020 is not the same. The people aren't the same and neither are the motivations it seems. So, if you're reading this and dating, I hear you, I feel you. I know it can be a mess. Finding an equally yoked partner is going to be hard and it's going to take some work. Know what's going to be even worse, if you don't take your time and put in the work? Getting caught up in feelings with an unequally yoked partner. The sexual chemistry is great but the future plans? Not so much. Or maybe there's a great future you can envision, but the personality is a no go. You feel irritated every time they speak? Been there, done that. It's not going to work.

This dating thing is like public transit. And just like real public transit, the dating train makes stops during its journey, and at times many stops. Some of these stops will be for you, some of them are for others. It's about knowing the difference of when you need to get on and off, another form of not every call deserves an answer. Just because the doors open doesn't mean this is the right destination for you. And then there are times it just passes right by certain stops when on a particular track, like an express train.

If your intention is to find a long-term partner, getting caught up may be a brief stop when you're realizing this ain't it, but eventually we get better at recognizing who is not equally yoked with us and don't even bother stopping.

Whether you are a believer or nonbeliever, religious or not, that's your business and not of importance. What I extracted from being equally yoked was the ability to work together and how important it is to find a partner that you can work together with, because partnership requires work. And when people have similar standards, expectations, and values, it makes it easier to work. Notice, I did not say what any of the standards, expectations, or values were or should be, because that's all personal preference. But what I am saying is that there is a correlation between like-minded people going at things together and being effective.

People who are caught up are not moving in the same direction or at the same pace. You are exactly that: caught, stopped too long, and you have to keep moving. How do you close the door and keep on moving? Align yourself to what you are looking for and make it swift. No second guessing yourself, you are by nature intuitive. Once you know what it is you want, it becomes easier to see situations for what they are. Maybe this stop is where you meet the love of your life or maybe it's a stop where you meet someone who loves your life and is making sure they are saying all the right things to be part of it.

Know the difference, sis.

It's with a foundation of what I value, understanding what matters to me, and years of applied observation (or being stopped too long one could say) that I created my Black Girl IRL Partner Rating System, "The List." This is my top-four list. Take what you need, leave what you don't, but most of all, come up with yours and starting rating!

BGIRLPRS Trait 1: Appearance

No ladies, not physical appearance. People will argue me down on this, but physical appearance cannot be the driving factor in establishing if you have a connection with someone. Physical appearances change. I think about how different I looked after each pregnancy and even after I recently had a physical injury.

Not only did my body change in different ways, so did my ability to "put myself together" on a day-to-day basis. During these times, some days were rough! The same for my husband. There have been times when we are juggling life, career, and kids that our physical appearance was not our priority. Other things had to get done instead of having a fresh line up or trim. That's what's real.

Physical appearance, assuming there are not any health issues being neglected, is a poor marker for success with a partner. I say this confidently because I've witnessed girlfriends go all the way in because someone was fine or had a six pack, and they ignored the red flags all around them. I'm not saying that if your partner has an interest in fitness or fashion, or if you both have a shared interest in both, that it's a bad thing. I'm saying that these interests are not the same thing as an interest in how someone looks. I have one friend in particular. From a physical appearance standpoint, she keeps herself together, always. Her dating stories are always the same. They always start off with, "OMG, I met this fine guy at the [insert any and every location]. His body was so nice."

Followed by, some weeks later, "I'm seeing [insert name of fine guy she met previously]."

More time passes: "He's so sweet and looks so hot every time I see him."

Still no real reference to anything he does beyond look hot.

Even more time passes: "I'm not sure [insert name of same hot fine guy] wants to settle down.

I think he just wants to have fun. He's just so fine though."

Now months and months have passed: "[Insert name of dude that just can't stop being hot] is cool, we hookup, but he's nothing serious. I'm open to dating other people since we don't have any titles."

And the cycle continues and continues.

For that reason, when I say appearance, I definitely don't mean looks. I mean appearance. Like, literally. Are they showing up for you over and over? Are they eager to be with you and vice versa? I needed someone that appeared. It might sound funny, but so many of my relationships before were with masters of the disappearing act. Dudes that appeared just enough to make it seem as though they were present, but in reality, they weren't there.

I remember an ex of mine was to attend my best friend's wedding with me. I was a bridesmaid. At the time, I lived out of state and so did he. That relationship in itself was rockier than the mountains in Colorado but nonetheless we were still going at the time of my friend's wedding. At least I thought we were. The week we were to fly to the wedding, we got in a big fight and didn't talk for days leading up to it. My flight and his weren't on the same day and we both had family in town. So I continued with the plans I thought we had.

My friend's wedding day comes around, I'm in town and doing my part as a bridesmaid. I stand in the front during the ceremony, look out briefly, and . . . there's no sign of him. The bridal party then heads from the ceremony to the reception in the bridal limousine. I'm thinking, "OK, he must have been lost in the crowd." This was an almost two hundred person wedding, after all. I take my seat at the head table and his seat is designated next to mine. I waited the entire reception; he never showed up. Our relationship ended that day. I stopped answering calls and changed any password on shared anything we had. The reality was he had not been appearing in our relationship for some time. His lack of appearance at the wedding just solidified what I already knew.

For me, appearance—the act of showing up— was number one on my list. And so, in order to keep things equal, if I felt that this wasn't a person I felt comfortable showing up for or I couldn't commit to doing that, then I knew it was a pass. On a scale of one to ten, I left no room in how much the urge to show up had to be. It needed to be a ten out of ten for both of us to work. Appearance, to this day, has been the driving force in how my husband and I navigate our marriage. It allows for each of us to be our limitless selves without fearing that the other person won't show up in support.

BGIRLPRS Trait 2: Money

Not how much money he has or even how much you have but how you both *treat* money. Listen, 22 percent of marriages end because of money issues and that's according to the Institute for Divorce Financial

Analysts.* Yes, there is an institute of people analyzing the financial causes for the end of marriages, it is that serious. So we gotta rock the same way with how we feel about money. We definitely can't be unequally yoked in our money mindset.

Now I acknowledge that people were raised and taught different things about money, and often that drives how people feel about money as adults. But I do know that I've done a certain amount of work and learning in regards to personal money management that I'd like my partner to have or at the least be open to adopting. We can't not see eye-to-eye on what's going to pay these bills and, more important, build generational wealth. Too many people get caught up in how much money their partner makes instead of how they spend their money. You ever know that man or woman who is always dripped out from head to toe in designer wear, but then come to find out they're behind on bills or on payment plans for things they do not need? My financial goals can't have me in the latest gear by any means necessary while I'm struggling to pay a light bill or a car note for a car that I need to get me to and from where I make money.

Sure, I've been attracted to people in the past immediately because of their career or financial status, and some of them have been, and still are, very nice people. But money alone does not make the person, and more important, how people manage

* "Survey: Certified Divorce Financial Analyst (CDFA) Professionals Reveal the Leading Causes of Divorce," IDFA, https://institutedfa .com/leading-causes-divorce.

all their money can be eye opening. It was watching other people manage, or rather not manage, their funds that made me realize that $10 - 20 = -10$, and no sir, I cannot live in the negative. I was observing people living what I considered extravagant lifestyles that were above their means just to keep up with the Diddys of the world—I couldn't sign on to that. If we are building a forever together, we need a forever that feels secure and stable even when things get rocky. Solid finances do that. And let me be clear, it's not about the quantity of money, it's about how whatever quantity is available in the relationship is treated. Do you value living within your means so that our day to day is not rocked by stressors of how we are going to afford the necessities? Are you happy with the lifestyle we can afford? Rich or poor, I want to know these things.

Money has power, they say. And I agree. It has the power to show me more about how you manage priorities and if you are willing to lean into what may be uncomfortable conversations with me. Or, like I said before, do you appear or disappear when it's time to get into these types of conversations? I'm not having these money conversations on the first date or even second, but once I know that we are heading down the route of seeing if we are willing to show up for each other through and through, then it's time to have the talk.

On the scale of importance, Money is an eight out of ten for me, and I sought people who matched that. They had an overarching concern for it, and if we weren't on the same page, there was a shared desire to get on the same page.

BGIRLPRS Trait 3: Height

You're probably seeing the trend here now. My required traits are not the traditional sense of the word but all still very valid. Height in my requirements wasn't physical height. Besides, the average height for the American male is five foot nine, so for all of you out there looking for six feet and up, much luck to you. I can't get too bogged down looking for genetic traits that are uncontrollable. I'm not sure how many people were given the choice of their height in the womb. I sure didn't choose mine so physical height can't be my choice for someone else.

So what do I mean by height? The height of their goals and aspirations. We have to be aligned. I'll put where that ranks on my scale up front, ten out of ten. I can't have this level of ambition and wanting to try every and anything to reach my goals and have you not want the same. I decided in my early thirties I was out of the project phase. What is the project phase? It's where if traits didn't match, or ambition in this case, I would be up for the project. I'd create experiences and exposure for them so that they would feel inclined to get on board.

Not used to this way of life or wanting these things for yourself? No worries, let me make sure I was going out of my way for you to understand why this is so important or essential to being the person I think you can be. I would basically be in a full-time relationship and a full-time project, a.k.a. job. I've edited resumes, applied for jobs, set up meetings, planned trips and adventures all to get people I was in a relationship with on the same page with what my hopes and aspirations were. Because to be honest, the way my personality is set up, I'm not OK with you observing from the sidelines either. That's just me.

I want you to be involved and on the same page. I now can see how these projects that masqueraded as relationships that I was in out of were unhealthy not only for me but for the other people as well. There's nothing healthy about pushing someone to be who they are not. Who they are and what they want out of life may not match up with your goals in life and that will have to be OK. You don't have to "fix" it. I think about how as Black women we may be set to the idea of scarcity being a real and true factor in us finding a long-term partner. We may fear being alone forever. I can say for sure my project phase was 100 percent a reflection of that—that feeling that if it didn't work with this person there wouldn't be anyone else coming after them. And that simply is not true.

I observe in my marriage now that often the output toward our goals ebbs and flows in support of the other so that we can have the overall bandwidth. Sometimes one of us is more motivated than the other, and that can be for various reasons. But what we are is always moving forward. I've known that from the start with my husband—our first date lasted seven hours because of that. We were busy talking about experiences had and to be had, things we've done and things we wanted to do. We didn't shy away from sharing those vulnerable "I hope to be able to" and "I'm working to be able to" conversations. There was comfort in sharing our goals.

When I was going out on dates with other people and trying to get a better idea of what they were about, I was instantly bored when the conversation was just about where they worked and what irked them or didn't irk them about their nine-to-five. I knew that my entrepreneurial heart needed more, and it wouldn't be fair for me to impose my spirit for independence from corporate America on them. I would have rather heard about what they were planning to do to escape the dependency on corporate life or a business or idea they had started or for that matter even failed. I wanted someone who also was willing to take the type of risk I would to get to the next point in life. And who undoubtedly knew they would encounter failure along the way and also would undoubtedly pick right back up and try again.

I noticed with people, if I told them about where I worked at the time as well as the business I was working on the side, they did one of two things; either ignored what I said completely about my side business as if it didn't exist and continued to talk about my corporate life, or they inquired more about what I was working on and the goals I had for that. The latter were my people. The ones that I felt more connected to. They understood that a business I chose to put my spare time and resources toward must have been something special to me. They sensed that the pursuit of that was what really made me tick. I didn't want to have to convince people of this. They had to pick this up on their own.

And there was a sense of understanding or like-ness. I ultimately landed on my husband being my person for that and other important reasons as well, but I can tell you that when a person really felt me and understood me like he did, the relationship was easy. When I got out of project mode and was not try-ing to force-connect things, I probably dated less as a side effect. There were a lot of early conversations and "talking" that ended quickly. Why waste the time or pick up more projects? But the people I did date and who were worth the next step were really, really aligned, and it came down to other factors for why it didn't work out.

Goals and aspirations just have to match, what-ever they are. No one defines what that match is but you. That is also to say that misaligned goals and aspirations do not mean that one is better than the other—this thought alone is what makes us go into project mode! We have to stop trying to fix someone or make them more like us. Sis, you have enough projects already and we already know we Black women are already exhausted. Making someone your project in a relationship can create resentment and contention, the exact opposite environment condu-cive for goal making and ambition seeking. Knowing what page someone is on early is helpful. Get that understanding that you need.

As I emphasize being aligned, understand that it doesn't have to be a narrow criteria. I like to be at the least on the same chapter as my partner. At times we may be off by a page or two—but we're flipping forward in the same general book and are aligned on what's next. The importance of this cannot be understated. So be mindful; don't let fear of never finding a partner or the perception of scarcity be a driving factor in not seeking this important alignment. The height of your ambition and your goals are deserving of being matched so that they can thrive, so that you and your partner can thrive.

BGIRLPRS Trait 4: Location, Location, Location

Just like in real estate, location matters. Ever been in a long-distance relationship? I have. Ever been in a long-distance relationship with no talk about not being a long-distance relationship? I have. All I'm saying is, don't tell me about the random couple you know that has been married for twenty-five years and commuted their whole marriage. That's good for them. What I know is 99.9 percent of long-term relationships are long term because of proximity. To me the long-distance relationship is the ultimate setup for "shit or get off the pot," excuse my language.

There's a genre of TV shows about couples making a decision about whether to continue or not continue their international long-distance relationship, à la *90 Day Fiancé*. Yes, they are also figuring out if the person is solely trying to get together for a green card or not in this show, but the reality is I'm not sure how many long-term relationships or marriages are lived across different countries. More than likely that's not going to be your story, sis, and for this trait, there is no workaround or alternate meaning.

The location matters.

I have been in and know other women who were in long-distance relationships for years. Years of figuring out the long-term intention, only to come to the conclusion that there is no intention because neither partner has a desire to relocate. Or the relationship was unable to get itself to the next step of commitment because it was void of the face-to-face time that was needed. I think of it like learning to ride a bike or swim; it's going to take the time it takes. And getting to commitment in a relationship is the same. For each relationship there's some time it will take, none of us know how long exactly, but what I do know is whatever time that is, distance doesn't make it shorter.

Where people live matters to them, and it should matter to you when you are dating. I am in no way against long-distance relationships, but I am speaking to the possibility of people staying together long term. I think people can meet people in different cities or even different countries, but if we are talking about having a life partner to have life experiences with, then the location in which that happens will eventually need to be the same. I know we may be inclined to overly depend on or want to substitute the role technology can play in facilitating shared experiences, but anyone who has argued with someone via text or a video call can tell you how so much meaning can be lost over technology.

When I first started my career in marketing the general rule of thumb based on research was that for the customer to buy something they had to be exposed to it between seven to eight times. That means we needed to have that bottle of fabric softener, as was the case for the brand I was working on, show up in some form or another in front of that customer at least seven times. We did this through commercials on TV shows we knew our target customers watched, ads in magazines they read, billboards and signage in the neighborhoods they lived, convenient shelf displays at the types of supermarkets they shopped at, and so on. All this to say, if a bottle of fabric softener needs to see you in person at least seven times for you to eventually take it home, you can imagine how many times and really how many hours another human being needs to interface with you for you to take them home (by which I mean commit to them long term; outside of that, you do you, if you know what I mean).

Technology, in a way, has set us back when it comes to the timeline relationships progress along. This is why presence can be forged with phone and video calls. It can appear that you are with the person all the time because, on a phone screen, you are. But when it comes down to it, the pheromones, the chemicals that the body produces to send signals to another, can't come through a phone screen. These in-person signals also aid communication.

Ever got pissed off at a text message because you made an assumption about the tone? I have. It sucks. Ever then see the person face to face and then have an awkward interaction but it eventually resolves or best of all it doesn't come up at all and your relationship continues on as usual? The point here is that technology can create a lot of suspended feelings and thoughts—not always, but sometimes and in relationships, from my experience, enough times. I mean, 90 percent of human communication is nonverbal.* Disagreements can fester for longer and misunderstandings can linger on without the full ability to see, touch, and hear someone in person.

Location will always be a ten out of ten, must be aligned for me. I was pretty particular up front that there were certain cities and locations that I just can't live in. If I'm with someone who just has to live in those places, we aren't a match. Sometimes I'm tempted to tell the friend that asks advice about the long-distance relationship to just quit it all together, because I'm so against it for myself since I know that is one area I am personally inflexible in. But I don't, since I do get it. The love of *your* life may not be in your hometown or the big city you moved to after college. Instead, I ask them, "What's the timeline?" When is this not going to be a long-distance

---

* "How Much of Communication Is Nonverbal?" UTPermian Basin, https://online.utpb.edu/about-us/articles/communication/how-much -of-communication-is-nonverbal.

relationship anymore, and what are the plans to make that happen? Those are the things I would consider if I were in their place.

I went to a wedding of a close friend recently and during the reception my husband and I were seated at the table with the groom's family. The groom's brother, also newly married, introduced us to his wife. She was really nice, and they seemed to have a really fun dynamic. We chatted most of the reception and even joined them on the dance floor a few times. They were people we definitely would be friends with if we lived in the same city.

One of our conversations that evening was where we each met our spouses. I started off by telling them how my husband and I met through an online dating app and how after the aforementioned seven-hour date, we both knew we had found our person. Surprisingly, or maybe not too surprisingly given the era we are in, they too had met on an online dating app. He was living in the United States and she was in the country she was born, raised, and lived in up until the point of their engagement.

I was immediately intrigued. I'd stumbled upon a real-life ninety-day fiancé, just like the show, I thought. So I started to ask more questions about the whole process and their dating story. It was all interesting and very similar to our story that when she knew, she knew. But what was the most interesting was the answer I got when I asked how they even met via app if they were living in different locations—this app in particular is location based.

The wife quickly spoke up and said, "I knew I wanted to live in the United States and had already visited my sister and mom here. I also knew that I was open to falling in love with anyone and that someone can potentially find their partner anywhere as long as they're open. So I made sure when I traveled to visit my sister and mom I turned my app on to go on dates." She also said, "What sense would it make for me to date someone in my home country if I knew I didn't want to live there?"

And while that may sound blunt—or scheming, depending on how cynical you are—sis in my opinion told no lies. She never said she was trying to marry any random person or be with someone who wasn't aligned with her values or her personal dating equation but she was clear that location mattered to her and that she needed to act and be intentional about where she dated. To me, if I'm not trying to live in Random-City-I-Do-Not-Ever-Want-To-Live-In I wasn't going to be dating there. With my luck I would have met the hometown hero or the city mayor and be forced into a lifetime of living somewhere I couldn't stand. Dating is already tough and can feel like mission impossible. Convincing someone that they should leave their forever home to come live in my forever home seems even tougher. More than likely, there's a list of things that will have to be disagreed and then agreed upon throughout the courting process, and I like easy wins. Location is an easy win in my book.

———

When I got clear on those four areas—Appearance, Money, Height, Location—I saw the people that were more aligned with what I wanted. There weren't tons of them, but they were there. If the fact that the dating pool seemingly drops is why so many of us don't get clear on our dating equation, then that's not a good enough reason. Besides, you can't spend the rest of your life with all of them anyways.

I wasn't trying to convince anyone to be anything they weren't or something that wasn't fair to them. I fundamentally knew where I was on the scale of the importance of my four areas, and I wanted someone who valued them the same—balance on both sides of the equal sign. Knowing that showing up for someone, having fundamental conversations on what would fuel our future, the goals that would get us there, and to be doing it together in the same place was my formula for successfully finding not just love, but partnership. I knew once those things were aligned all that was left was that magical feeling of connection. That can't be quantified or predicted but what I do know is that it does come along at the right time.

I recognize that me saying that your match will come along at the right time, as a person on the other side of finding their match and now in a committed relationship that has resulted in marriage, may sound trite. Even more so when I know that some of the most deserving people of companionship, Black girls in real life, are still (and at times it may feel more like, STILL!) waiting for that right someone to come along at the right time. I know you have been using or will use your own BGIRLPRS type system and the math will still not be mathing. The wait can and will feel like forever—months or even years at times. The feeling of time running out can also seem more daunting for us Black girls as we reach milestones in other parts of our lives.

To say it can feel rough to hear "keep waiting" is an understatement. I remember hearing "Your time will come" from some friends, along with the "maybe you're too picky" from others. As if my wait was being prolonged by wanting the things that were important to me. So many times, I wanted to go all in on the situationship, hoping something magical would turn it into a real relationship, because at least then I wouldn't be alone or have to throw my expectations of a partner out the window. I was doing the work, so why not find someone that I could help do the work too? Then I would snap out of it and remind myself: no sis, that's a project, and at this point in your Black girl life as you're seeking true partnership you don't have time for projects.

I've been there and contemplated it all. I've showed up as the bridesmaid in friend after friend's wedding or opted to bring my mom as my plus-one because I definitely couldn't let Mr. Wrong think this was the path that we could be headed down. That's why I have to be real with you, I'm going to say the same thing that you've already heard, the dreaded statement: "Your time will come." You're going to have to keep waiting. I cringe saying it, since it's one of the toughest parts of being a Black woman, knowing that for some things our wait may be longer than our peers. Even more so, the process of finding the one for us can be an added stressor in our lives that are already stressful enough. But what I can do is reframe the wait with you.

Do you trust yourself? I hope you do. You've trusted yourself thus far to go after the things that you went after and to make the decisions in every other part of your life that have made you the fabulous Black girl that you are. Whether that trust was there from the beginning or from years of learning and improving on who you are, rest assured that you can rely on it. You've already relied on it to reach your other nonrelationship goals. Do you trust what you want for yourself? I hope that is a resounding yes. Because you trust yourself, you know what you want for yourself.

You, Black girl, know that what you want for yourself is nothing less than wonderful.

The person you are today is the manifestation of all of those things that you want and have wanted for yourself. Your relationship will be the same. It shouldn't be anything less than wonderful with the person that checks all your boxes or, as we call it, your personal BGIRLPRS. When your time comes, your partner will reflect the trust you have in yourself and the things you want. In the meantime, the wait is a reflection of your trust in yourself. It reflects that you are willing to trust yourself and wait for someone who aligns to your needs and desires in your partner and vice versa. Everyone who has come your way during the wait and wasn't the one really just affirms that you know what you want and you're not willing to settle or cut the time short.

When I say I was tempted to cut my time short, it never sat well with who I knew myself to be or what I wanted. It's easy to conflate the situationship you may have gotten caught up in into a real relationship, especially when you get tired of waiting, but girl, don't do it. It's funny now that I'm married to someone who likes to repeat "It takes the time it takes" whenever I get frustrated about something that relates to time. It's ironic because I got married "late," whatever that means. But it did take the time it took. Looking back, I wouldn't—or rather, I couldn't—be married a day earlier than I was married. I needed that time to learn and solidify who I was. To be able to enter into a marriage as a whole person and not someone who was in a rush to be completed by someone else. The time is going to pass regardless, because like my husband tells me, "It takes the time it takes."

Trust yourself during that time and get firm on who you know yourself to be. Double down on that trust. In fact, celebrate it. Learn more about who you are and what you want during this time of wait. Refine your BGIRLPRS as you get even more clear on those things and keep applying it to potential matches. And if it doesn't fit, keep the dating train moving.

We're only stopping when it's a match!

Truth #4

You May Be the Side Chick, Rebound, or Other Nonpriority Role

I once went to a medium and she immediately looked up at me and told me that I had a calling. Before she even began her work, she said, "You can feel people. You should work on your craft." I was skeptical about mediums before I went there, but the whole thing was part of a total mind-body experience that I'd paid for, so I figured what did I have to lose. But I knew what she was really picking up was my Black girl intuition. That feeling that when shit ain't right, it ain't right. That "I don't need anyone to try to convince me otherwise, something is going *on* here" feeling.

We have some of the best intuition I've ever seen. A Black woman will tell you straight up "I don't mess with So-'n'-So," and are able to offer no explanation as to why. Then, out of nowhere, when So-'n'-So gets caught up into something, the Black woman will give you that knowing look, like "I told you so." Let me tell you, as a result of Black women's intuition, there are whole stores, streets, parks, neighborhoods, or just places that Black people don't go. Their momma told them growing up that they don't need to be there because they just don't get a good vibe from it. So these things, people, places, situations, the avoidance is just going to be what it is; I'm not testing it out or trying to see if we get on better next time, I'm good.

That feeling you get, and you know exactly what it is, makes you start rolling your eyes and twitching a little when someone shares a story with you about something that just doesn't seem quite right. As Black women we are always receiving information, processing it, and trying to figure out if we should say something or not. You know, is this a moment to be silent or not? Should I just respectfully nod, or F-it, I'm gonna say something. It is hard. And in friendships and relationships and discussing relationships with those friends, sometimes you don't know whether you should protect your girl or just tell her the truth. Should you stay quiet or let it be a lesson learned?

I think everyone appreciates having that friend that has that no-questions-asked level of commitment to the friendship. I try to be that no-questions-asked type of friend who listens to every and anything and provides a safe space for the wildest stories and the most transparent of feelings to be heard. I'm also blunt, so when *I* know that *you* know that we *both* know that your relationship is suspect, I'm going to say something, girl. You've got other friends that will sugarcoat things for you.

I'm most compelled to speak up when I know for sure someone has found themselves in the oh so dreadful side chick, other chick, whatever chick, not the main chick situation. And let me tell you, I've seen it and been it. Time after time, ladies, we see the signs and continue on, and it's time to call them out so we can stop the madness. Settle for no other position than the main and priority, if that's what we are seeking.

Because, ladies, despite all that work you did to find the one, there's some telltale signs that you're not a main player in the game, you're an alternate. It's hard to admit, but we've all been there at some point or another. Let's just talk about it for a moment so we don't get ourselves into that situation again.

I'll start off by saying that if it looks a mess, and smells like a mess, then it's probably a mess. Whether you are observing from the outside or inside one of those relationships—you know, they know, we all be knowing—it's a hot mess! Twice in my life I have been that person. Looking back I cringe thinking about it, and even more cringeworthy is how obvious it was. Some people will say it was because I was young but I'd say it goes back to the feeling of scarcity and the want to keep these project-like relationships around for fear of never finding someone else.

I think at times I subconsciously and other times blatantly in all consciousness denied what I knew. That I was the side piece, the rebound, or whatever I was, I clearly was not the main one. I actively turned my intuition off to try to force the outcome I wanted. I recognize that sometimes admitting you're in a bad situation can feel worse than continuing on in a bad situation. The embarrassment makes you keep it up, at least that's how I felt. I have rebounded from one foolish situation to the next. Yes, you don't always learn on the first try, but I'm going to put it out there, ladies. Learn from me.

First rule: you are no Max or Nev. If you feel the need to launch into your own *Catfish*-style investigation or engage your friends to do so with you, leave it alone, sis. I don't know at what point a relationship feels good when you have to go snooping, investigating, or trying to piece together clues as to why something is up. I'm not talking about just light insecurity or disbelief, that may be normal—like the feeling this could be too good to be true, or a one-off incident that you addressed and the person was forthcoming with information and willing to resolve it. I'm talking about the constant "something ain't right" feeling that forces you to become the detective you know you aren't.

Depending on which friend it is, I know that if I get that one-word text message "Gail," that means get the dark glasses and the walkie-talkies because we are about to go out on a mission, don't ask no questions. I know that I need to get suited up. While I kid, I know you *know* what I'm talking about. That Black girl bat signal we like to send out whenever we feel like we need help snooping or doing some investigation. Whether it's one word or a few words, it usually comes in the form of a text message or call and is completely random. Well, if you didn't hear me before, I'm saying it again: girl, stop. No need to go on the see-whose-pictures-he's-commenting-on,

*69-blocked-caller-ID, wait-until-he's-asleep-to-check-his-phone type of investigation. If you can't openly and respectfully discuss your concern with your partner, is this the type of relationship you want to be in in the first place?

For me, it wasn't. I had to hard pause and evaluate my need to get to the bottom of what I already knew when I found myself on stakeout. Yes, a stakeout. Judge me if you want but we all have had a stakeout-like moment in our life somewhere. Of course, my Black girl intuition knew that—let's just call him Mr. Wonderful—was up to something. And after one too many evenings of my gut telling me something just wasn't right, I found myself making a "Girl you need to come over right now" call to one of my good friends. And she understood the assignment. Before I even hung up the phone, we already knew what we were going to do. Like the two Black girls on a mission to find what we knew we were already going to find, we set out on a stakeout.

The whole thing was a mess, and forty-five minutes in, I started getting antsy. This was definitely not my chosen profession. And as fate would have it, because God really must have wanted me to know I needed to stop this, just as we were about to abandon the mission, the truth showed its face. I saw what I needed to see, another girl outside of his apartment, as we set out to leave. Not only was I immediately embarrassed, I was sad to actually be right with my intuition. But like I said, we be knowing. Doing all that was a waste of time, and I'm telling you too, Black girls who think they too should become super sleuths, don't waste your time. We already talked about all the other stuff we have going on. Do we really have the time to be in a relationship that requires this level of checks at any time? My take on it is this: reserve the cheating and scandal-solving to the TV shows. When they do it, it's entertainment. When you do it, it's an emotional time suck you don't need. If you have to become a detective in your relationship, is it really a relationship?

Second rule: If there are no clear titles, I don't know if you are in what you say you are in. For me, that is what it is. People can debate me all day long on why titles aren't necessary, and I'm going to tell them to go to an untitled doctor. They won't. There is a needed amount of time and work in order to get that Dr. that then makes that person presumably qualified to take care of you. Same goes for relationships. Show me a multiyear relationship with no titles and I'm going to venture to say that you're not the priority in that relationship. The time is there but the work—meaning the ability to prioritize you—just isn't.

You know what I didn't do before I went on that stakeout to Mr. Wonderful's apartment? Clarify what the hell we were. I think I was so scared to hear what we weren't, I didn't bother. I assumed all the time we were spending together made it obvious that we were together, but it did not.

Many of us mistake someone's showing up like a boyfriend, girlfriend, or a committed partner for actually *being* one of those things. I've rationalized the necessity to find this out down to this: if it's important to you and it is something that you want to be, then you should find out if that's what you are, if it has not been clearly stated. How many of us have that friend who thinks she's in a relationship and obviously is not? I do. The telltale signs are all there but the most tellingest—in my made-up Black auntie word—of signs is that she don't got no title. That they've been dating for the better part of a year or more and titles "aren't important." Turn around a month or even another long-wasted year later and she, or you if it's you, are still waiting around for the next step in the relationship. How can we get to the next step if the first step doesn't even have a definition? A title? How are we going from nothing to engaged or even married? So I stick by it: no title, no relationship.

Third rule: If they're missing in action for significant time blocks, you ain't the main one. Before we get all accusatory here, let's not count the time block of legit hanging with friends, work, and travel or travel for work. Let's also not get to into the details of needing to know their whereabouts every minute on the minute. That would be too much and not realistic. What I'm saying is obvious things: if you can't get in contact or have not been in communication for days at a time, or let's say consistently at certain times of the day when they are not doing any of the above things, then Houston we have a problem.

In my case, Mr. Wonderful went missing every night at certain times, despite us spending so much time together. We didn't live together so that assisted whatever side doings was going on, but looking back, it was obvious. And before you do that intuitive eye roll, like girl, duh, know that like I said before, I knew I ignored my intuition because that was not the outcome I wanted to be true.

We do not need to GPS our partners. I repeat, we do not have to GPS our partners. But when the relationship gets to a certain place, (see Rule 2 about those titles) we both need to have a general awareness of each other's time blocks throughout the day. When you are the priority in someone's life, you know these things about them and they know these things about you because you seek opportunities to be together, not avoid each other. And generally speaking, if you do progress to living together or marriage and a family if that is your choice, these time blocks are going to matter as you plan a life together that depends on each other. Not knowing what is going on with your partner for significant stretches of time, or your partner only showing up during certain times, is the exact opposite of commitment. That is just what is convenient for them.

So many times I've heard Black women overlook this whole fleeting availability their partners exhibit and pass it off as "busy." I'm not saying they are not busy, but missing in action with no call back or, even worse, no explanation is not "busy" in my books. It's shady. Destiny's Child didn't title their hit "Say My Name" because this is uncommon behavior when game may be being run. "Say my name, if no one is around you" (wherever you supposedly are that is), "Say my name, you acting kind of shady" (because we all know what is really going on).

Fourth and last rule: If there's casual behavior in the middle of the chaos, chances are there's an inability to commit in general. Let me explain. When I finally caught up with Mr. Wonderful after my stakeout and had the opportunity to confront him, I didn't the first time. I was still embarrassed and in disbelief. But when I finally came around and did so, you'd think it wasn't a big deal.

I'll say refer back to rules one through three again to see how we got to this point, but really rule two and three are why it wasn't a big deal to him and, honestly, shouldn't have been to me if I was paying attention. We had no clear titles and he was missing consistently enough.

"Who said we were in something serious?" he asked.

"Oh, hmmm," I managed to embarrassingly mumble out.

I just assumed we were, I thought. Wrong. And even though I didn't vocalize the thought, he could see it on my face. I felt like a dummy. And him? He felt like nothing significant had happened. People that are so casual in situations in which they are "caught" or that could be interpreted as "revealing" to me are not ready to commit to anyone being the priority at that time. Life and relationships are just as casual as their response, and you don't have to stick around for it, especially if that is not what you want. If you don't want to be someone's casual hookup or sidepiece or rebound or nonserious relationship, then you don't have to be. You make clear your expectations (that includes the title you want *ahem*) and if they aren't on board with that, you leave.

For me, there have been several times where I feared loneliness. As a Black woman, I feared I would never find the one or that I would be by myself in times when everyone else would have someone. I thought about all of us Black women "they" said never got married, or all the reasons "they" say we won't have children. And because of that, I stayed in situationships and not-so-ideal situations. Situations that my Black girl sixth sense told me instantly were no good, but I ignored it. But you know what I noticed? During that time of staying, I felt more alone. I felt like I was by myself and besides myself, because my real self knew better. I kept justifying what didn't make sense.

So how does one get out of the cycle? Well, for one, start small. Start by believing what you see. If it doesn't add up, then it's not for you. Don't wait around for it to make sense, because it won't. We're in a relationship, but your availability is sporadic at best, and there's no job, real reason, or evidence as to why? Next. You already know we're exhausted, sis. No need to use more of the time you already don't have to figure it out. Are there tons of phone conversations but never a real effort to meet in person? Next. You're not marrying an iPhone. Do you feel like you've taken on a new job just from the constant investigating you have to do to figure out what's going on? Please stop. Reclaim your time and become more comfortable with being alone. Yes, you heard me, alone. Not lonely but by yourself. If you can't stand being by yourself, why would anyone else want to be with you? Why are we so afraid to spend time with ourselves and our thoughts? So much so we'd rather be someone's option indefinitely?

I've had to dig deep into those questions even with my therapist more recently for life in general. What is it that we are willing to settle for so we don't feel bored? As I pulled myself out of my own situationships, I knew that being alone wasn't going to kill me.

You know what time alone did for me? It allowed me to get deeper into understanding who I was as a person. It also allowed me to stop letting a bad use of my time, like these pseudo relationships, mask who I truly was out of fear of being by myself. By myself, I was clear on who I wanted to be and who I wanted to be with. While I dated with intention, what I gained from not needing to be in every and any relationship were intentional gaps. Time I used to do things I like to do alone or with full focus. This time I was the side chick to none and the priority to the most important person: me. I wish the same insight and clarity to all my Black girls in real life. Embracing who we are, the most important person to ourselves, and being treated as a priority at all times by the person we choose to share our lives with.

Truth #5

Sometimes You'll Lose Your Ride or Die

Sisters. At least, that's what we told people we were.

We shared birthdays. Not on paper, but in the bond we had. After twenty-something years of friendship, we might as well have been family. Maybe that's why I didn't see it coming. In hindsight it had probably been a year of me reaching out and doing all the first calling, messaging, planning the meetups. I am a planner and nurturer by nature so it didn't immediately feel that out of the ordinary. But it wasn't until Christmas came and went that one fateful year that I realized it was all falling apart. There wasn't a text, an email, or anything from my Best Friend that entire year.

There are a good number of friends I've grown to expect just an occasional check-in every so often, and who have also grown to expect the same from me, but in my midthirties I could never have imagined losing a lifelong friendship. It hit hard. I'd always assumed friendships, like romantic relationships, needed some big thing to happen for them to end—but they don't.

I became friends with my Best Friend at fifteen, and who we were then definitely wasn't who we grew up to be later in life. We were so much alike as teenagers but so different as adults. More and more our paths clearly were diverging. The ghosting that ultimately confirmed the end of our friendship was actually the gentlest way that a friendship like that could have ended. That friendship spanned more years than any other relationship I had outside of family. But the moments of shared enjoyment of each other's company had become fewer and fewer, and we were clearly only bonded by time.

The loss of that friendship wounded me, much more than I thought it would, and was very different than a romantic relationship ending. There can be a lot of ego and possessiveness in friendship, especially among Black women. Our possessiveness lets us hold each other down no matter what, because I've got your back. And that ego, it's what keeps us focused and driven because there ain't no way we're going to be the only one in the crew not showing up in life as our best self. As you can see, I mean them as good things. However, if that friendship ends, you may end up like I did, with that ego bruised and asking questions like: Why would someone not want to be friends with me? Who else are they going to be friends with? Or the petty, I hope she doesn't show up at So-'n'-So's party tonight.

By choice, most of my besties are Black and Brown women. I just connect well with them. It's the built-in shared understanding of experiences that only we are forced to navigate daily that does it for me. The easiness of those friendships has been vital to me, especially during the times that life comes at you in a not-so-easy way. It's not to say that I do not or have not made an effort to connect with women outside of my race or culture, I do. But when my friendship with my Best Friend ended, a fellow Black girl IRL, it made the end feel even worse. Black girls are supposed to stick together, right? We don't just fall apart. It had the not so good parts of my ego and possessiveness kicking into overdrive. What I learned navigating that whole situation was acceptance, because, look, that's what you have to do when you lose your ride or die. You just have to.

My parents are Black, immigrants, and baby boomers—the triple threat in raising kids destined for therapy. I know there are probably a lot of us kids of these parents probably still processing to this day. What I do know is that for my parents, having the time to devote to friendships the way I devote my time to friendships would have significantly changed the outcome of their lives. Friendships like I have now, at the same age they were then, were a luxury they couldn't afford; they would have been a burden. Friendships that overindexed on joy were for the rich, the established, not my people. Not my parents. My parents spent more time working to achieve the American dream and making sure my sister and I could have the time and resources for those types of time-consuming friendships. They didn't have time to take breaks with their peers just for happiness. Their definition of a social life was clearly defined; see your family during holidays and birthdays (thankfully they both had more than five siblings so no family gathering lacked people or activity) or talk to other adults at church (my mom only), or maybe just talk to people at work. That was what friendships looked like for my parents.

So, when I began to "make friends" it was much more than just making friends. It was me finding community with other people, mostly other Black and Brown first-generation Americans, who also didn't see a lot of friendships rooted in fun, enjoyment, or shared experiences. My first friends and I created the connections we craved. Losing a friend, my best friend at that, for the first time was a shake-up of my whole friendship infrastructure. This was a relationship built on support, happiness, and enjoyment. And let me tell you, as a Black woman navigating those emotions, this type of friendship ending was tough. I barely had the bandwidth to manage my thoughts on other things and here I was managing the biggest breakup I've ever had, period. I got over it (I'll tell you how in a moment) and continued growing because of it. But yes girl, I've been there too. Hopefully some of my thoughts on it can help you grow through it too, if you've ever experienced the same.

First off and most important, as blunt as it sounds, accept that the friendship is done. Whether or not you truly want to accept it, you must. Just like we intuitively know things about relationships, we know at this point in your life when a friendship has reached its end. Whether it was a nasty argument (which I hope not, but it happens) or a year plus of no communication like I experienced, you know when there's no more life left in a friendship. When the effort to resuscitate the friendship is work that you do not want to do, and choose not to do because the outcome doesn't lead to the life you want to live, you may have to let that friendship go. The faster we accept that losing that girlfriend, that sis, that fellow Black Girl in Real Life that you couldn't imagine not knowing, the faster we can heal and move forward with the benefits of losing a friendship. (Yes, I said benefits. More on that to come too.)

In just about every recovery program, as well as what I'm suggesting here about navigating friendships coming to an end, acceptance is part of the process. In mostly all of those programs, acceptance is the last step. But I'm saying let's do that part first. Let us use the recognition of acceptance to ultimately, over time, truly understand and accept that that friendship has come to an end. It's important because we can't control a lot of aspects of what caused a friendship to end. There may have been aspects like our own behavior or responses that we do have control over, but what the other person says and does is out of our hands. I know for me this is the first place my ego showed up, questions around why would someone not want to be friends with me? I wanted to be in control of the separation and to make sure that none of our other friends heard things about me that were not true. My hesitance to accept was more about wanting to control the story about why it came to an end than the actual ending itself.

Have you found yourself in that situation before? Seemingly grieving the end of a friendship or relationship, the one that felt like it could be forever, but your thoughts tend to circle around the narrative? Accept the occurrence and spend less time on the narrative. That part is also less controllable than you think.

Which brings me to my second point, things that are said about you are not your business. Anytime I express to my therapist some thought or concern about what other people may have said about me or may be saying about me, she always responds, "So what?" The first few times she asked this, it was really jarring. Like, "Girl, who are you talking to?" To this day, it still catches me by surprise every now and then when she says it. But over time, what I learned she was really saying is "it is what it is." So what if someone, and in this case your former friend, talks bad about you? So what if you're the topic of conversation in the friend group, even the villain perhaps? So what, because what fundamentally changes about you as a result of this?

Nothing.

I had months of pent-up fear thinking: What would my ex-friend be saying about me? Who would she be saying it to? How would other friends that we have in common think about me when our friendship ended? And all of it didn't matter. I know who I am, and I hope you do too. I know what is important to me and what drives me. I know that as long as I am operating as who I am authentically, whatever anyone else has to say about me is none of my business. In fact, any conversations that may be going on about me without me are entirely their business, not mine. Those conversations are more about how that person may be healing, venting, seeking reassurance or even entertainment, as in the case of gossip. Those conversations have never really been about me.

After over a dozen "so whats" in therapy, I finally am in a place of not trying to figure things out or track down the conversations that could be going on about me. It is a waste of my time to do so, and nothing is gained when you do track or uncover what it is you are looking for. Besides, have you ever confronted someone about talking behind your back before? Most of the time that doesn't go well, and rarely are you getting the answer you are looking for in that confrontation. And who can blame the person? It doesn't feel great to be "caught" being unpleasant. Well, wasting time trying to track down what could be being said about you is just another form of confronting people. When you are confronting every source, conduit, observer of the information you think is out there, just like confronting someone face to face, rarely does that go well. Get comfortable with not only accepting that the friendship has come to an end, but that the ending of the friendship and aspects about you that may be discussed by the other person is, guess what? None of your business.

Sometimes we just don't get closure.

What I used to find most unsettling about my friendship with my best friend falling apart, or rather ghosting apart, is that to this day I have no idea why it really happened. I mean I went from ride or die to did she die? How come I haven't heard from her in so long? I had no firm ending of the friendship for myself until I accepted it was over and started to move on. And yes, I could have reached out to clarify or understand what was going on but there was evidence with other friends we had in common that my ex-friend was still choosing to be in those friendships but it was ours that was no longer a fit. Knowing the specifics of why someone chooses to not be friends with you or why your friendship is not working is one of those things we are going to have to let go. There's peace in not having to know.

Plus, how many times does a rough day make you not the happiest and most cheerful Black girl on the block? That's certainly been me enough times. So many things going on in our lives simultaneously affect how we interact with other people, let alone our friends and loved ones. Also, we are Black women, so we know so much is going on outside of just us, always. I know me, if I'm irritated, tired, stressed, or dare I say hungry, I'm not the one. If the conversation needs extra levels of compassion and it's not life or death, I'm going to have to avoid it. That may show up like me purposely missing your call or not answering a text or even canceling plans we've had for weeks. These responses have nothing to do with the person or friend they may affect, and everything to do with how I protect my peace. I think similarly other people, our friends, are going through so much of their own stuff that, sometimes, decisions to not continue a friendship is best for them and, in turn, protects their peace and the respect that was there.

Maybe to someone you're the friend who requires a lot of engagement and they no longer have the bandwidth to sustain that, given whatever else is going on in their lives. Maybe even for you, you find yourself constantly comparing yourself to a friend to the point it is unhealthy to maintain that friendship. You may even experience a positive growth in a new direction that makes you feel that a different friend or group of friends can better support that. I've personally had that feeling and responded to it without feeling guilty about it in recent times. Every explanation for friendship incompatibility isn't needed. It can occur and you can accept it, sometimes never knowing why, but do not try to control the narrative.

You know what often creates the hesitance in living this way when it comes to navigating the next steps after ending or losing a friendship? The same feeling of scarcity that we Black women experience in dating. The fear that another best friend, another perfect match of a person, will never come around. That feeling that there's a limited selection of people that we can vibe with and no more will come along. And just like in dating, that's just not true. We can set the same clear expectations for the type of friendships we are looking for and do the things that help us get those friendships. Want a friend who is caring and a good listener? Be the listener you are looking for in someone else. Want to find friends? Just like dating, try friendships with different people. Take coffee dates, meet up at events, call people you think may have similar interests. Some may work and some may not. To find friendship as an adult is a whole task we have to commit to, but you must show yourself as friendly in order for friends to find you.

Last, losing your ride or die, your BFF, or even just a friendship that lasted for a long time that you didn't expect to lose, can cause true grief and sadness and we should lean into that. The feelings that really suck about the whole situation are real and shouldn't be avoided. So often, as Black women, we are forced to put on that tough exterior and play the role that things don't affect as. Especially a thing like this, losing a part of our close support system—a member of our community—but it has an impact emotionally. But what I know about us is, our friendships, when we are in them, are solid pieces of work. Black women together are powerhouses, so the ending of our friendships are momentous and do deserve the momentous grief that comes when that happens.

I, for one, felt sadder than I'd felt for any romantic breakup when I accepted my friendship with my best friend was over. In a lot of ways, it felt like a death had occurred. There were no more phone calls to be had (despite them not happening for over a year at the point it ended), no more random happy hour meetups, and no one who appreciated celebrating my birthday and her birthday like they were both truly ours together. But just like grief, the feeling of the loss of the friendship is not meant to disappear; it will be there day in and day out. It will take up a lot of space in the beginning and over time, slowly, take up less and less space. Call it my inclination toward feeling anxious in social settings, but in the first few weeks after I'd accepted that my friendship was over, I was so fearful I might run into my ex-friend somewhere. Nothing had changed from one day to the next, because she and I hadn't spoken for a year at that point, but the acceptance and awareness alone shifted how I started to feel. I had to accept that I felt sad and scared. I went from feelings of hope that there was just some yearlong misunderstanding to thinking "I hope I don't see her." Those feelings of extreme fear eventually subsided as I processed my acceptance and "So what?" proclamations as well as being fine not knowing the cause of the end.

Now I'm not looking for friendships to end, but I'm open to finding the types of friendship that are better suited to the continuously evolving me. I hope you are too. Friendships may end just for that reason alone, to make way for your Black Girl Magic (wink) to really shine. Maybe the next version of your life needs a different type of support system, or you are going to be able to support your friends in a new way given where you are at now. Maybe the circle of friends you need in order to maintain that healthy competition to keep up with the goals you have looks different from the past but is more aligned with who you are.

Whenever I get stuck in the thoughts of loss, I ask myself, your ride or die may no longer be there, but did you ever only need just that one friendship? Of course, I didn't. I'm so much more than one relationship. Were you not who you were before that? That I was and that I am. And isn't who you are now even more fabulous, sis?

Yes, yes it is.

Truth #6

Therapy Is a Journey

The views in this chapter do not come from a medical provider. They come from me, a Black girl in real life. My views and experiences are in no way a substitute for seeking out your own advice, diagnosis, or treatment from a mental health provider. And although the process in this chapter is truly a process, you should in no way delay seeking care or disregard advice when it comes to your mental health because it is taking more time and/or work than you planned for. If at any time you are having a mental health emergency, please call your doctor or emergency services immediately.

I feel like there was no such thing as a therapist before 1999. I mean, I know in *theory* therapists existed. But in terms of things that changed Black people's lives in the 2000s, the list would go: iPhone, Black social media, *Black Panther*, and Black people talking about therapy. I'm sure people always went to therapy, but my people, Black people, going to therapy and talking about therapy, this isn't just new. It's *new* new. That's the new, so fresh thing people can't wait to get their hands on it. That, if you haven't experienced it yet, you must be missing out.

I remember when I first felt "left out" of therapy. The FOMO was real. My friend was chatting about a disagreement she and her then partner had and how her therapist (whom she just mentioned casually) had really helped her not react the same way that she used to. I knew exactly what my friend was talking about when she said "how she used to act" because in the past I'd gotten so many of those "Girl, you better come get me 'cause it's not going to be good" calls from her, I'd lost count. And usually, if I could get away with not having to leave my house, I would put her on hold quickly and return with all four of the bestie crew on the phone ready to do a group intervention to calm her down. So to hear her talk about one of those situations, and how she resolved it without having to be picked up or an all-hands-on-deck phone mediation that involved a mix of laughter, tears, and come-to-Jesus moments, I knew that therapy was something that worked.

It's the casual conversations about therapy among my friends that makes me feel like therapy isn't just for the bad times or the tough times. It's for all times. Even the good times, especially the "life is flourishing" times. Imagine if we only went to the gym when we wanted to lose weight? I mean people can do that *ahem* and may have tried to do that *cough cough* (it's me; I'm people) but that's not the optimal way to keep our bodies functioning. Ideally, a consistently healthy diet and an active lifestyle is our best bet at remaining the healthiest. The better we get at the consistency, the less we have to *ahem* run off that overdoing it pizza session we had the night before. That's how I feel about therapy at all times, not just sometimes. The consistency helps me better manage the highs and lows of life. And when those mental pizza moments happen (i.e., when I get so overwhelmed by my thoughts, I can't seem to function in the moment), I'm not searching for the quick fix.

Finding a therapist, though, is much like dating; there are qualities about the type of therapy and the therapist that must work for you. There needs to be a match. And although we're probably not looking for our equally yoked therapist and the same type of math that we use in the Black Girl IRL Partner Rating System, there is some connection or quality that resonates with you that you're going to need. For everyone those things will be different, there's no one way to approach it, but because therapy requires so much vulnerability on our part, I think it makes sense to absolutely consider what those things may be as you embark on your search. Or even as you go through therapists as I did, things may come to you or resonate with you while you're in the middle of the process that make you readjust your criteria, and that is OK. This is to say that approaching therapy doesn't have to be met as a race to find the right therapist immediately. It took a long time to make you who you are today, so taking the time to consider who you'd like to share all those parts of yourself that has taken so much time to craft is a perfectly good way to approach finding your therapist match.

Nonetheless, my therapy FOMO ended right after I had my first panic attack. I no longer felt like I was making up an excuse to need therapy or had to dig very deep to explain why I was seeking out therapy, if asked. As part of my recovery plan I created for myself, I sought out a therapist who specializes in anxiety and panic attacks. This part of my therapy journey is what I call the "I need to fix this" approach to therapy.

The urgency I had is what so many overwhelmed and panic-attacked women have experienced. It's urgent because we definitely couldn't bring ourselves to therapy before (read: generational shame about the whole thing). If I'm being honest, I'm still not sure how much of my immediate family knows that I have a therapist. Maybe it's part "it's my business; I can share when I want to share" and part the lingering effects of generational shame. Even now in my family, if it is mentioned that someone goes to therapy, it can be a bit of a joking matter about the reasons the person needs therapy or how, in their opinion, it clearly isn't working. I know that wrapped in their jokes about therapy is their own lack of experience and maybe even fears about judgment, if they too went to therapy. So many of us, like myself initially, hesitate to begin therapy even when it becomes urgent because of the opinions or comments of those close to us.

I'm not going to lie, it is a big step to actually even begin the process of finding a therapist. I'm not talking about vetting a therapist you've already found, which I will talk about later in this chapter. I'm talking about picking up the phone and actually making an appointment. What's worse than calling around and making that first appointment? Filling out one of those online forms where you have to leave your email address or phone number for them to call you back. Why do I need to now fret that you, the therapist, are going to call me back at the most inopportune time? It will be when I'm out with friends or around coworkers and the call will come and we'll have to go into a deep dive of why I need therapy.

These were the thoughts that, for a long time, kept me from even initiating the search. It felt like the first part was "How do I keep the secret of wanting to find a therapist even in the search?" I don't want to ignore how many of us experience this hesitance that leaves us stuck for some time. You may even be stuck right now. The struggle can be real, but the need can be even greater.

Think about how many things you may have struggled to begin in the past (hello procrastination!), and then when you finally get it done, it wasn't that big of a deal. That's how I feel about getting started on the search for a therapist. If you're on the fence about it, I hope you know that we've all been in a similar place in regard to how to get started. Personally, outside of affirming to myself that this was a task I was going to complete, I also did not put pressure on myself for when it had to be done by. If after I filled out one of those dreaded online inquiry forms I got a call back at a not-so-great time or an email while my plate was already full, I told myself I could call back or respond when it was a good time for *me*. No pressure to pick up right away and awkwardly conceal the conversation that was being had. For me, a good time to take a call or reply to an email was in my office when I had scheduled downtime and knew that I would be mentally present to do so. I knew it wasn't a good time when I was out and about or trying to tend to things with the family or my kids.

The biggest improvement I found in getting over the hump to get started was how I spoke to myself about therapy. What narrative was I authoring about what therapy is for me? Therapy for me and for many of us Black girls IRL is another tool that improves our lives. We always want to be the best version of ourselves, and just like other things that I do to enable that—like getting help around the house, going to the gym, or bingeing cheesy Netflix romantic comedies—therapy also had a place. It may not be the choice that the people around me are using to improve their lives, but we don't all have or use the same tools when it comes to choosing what works for us.

Most if not all of my feelings about starting therapy were centered around those two things: timing and what it said about me. These were two things that I could control with my approach. Sis, maybe some of the hesitance you are having about taking the step to consider therapy can be controlled in how you approach it. Maybe starting therapy returns more positive value to your life than the time you spend contemplating starting it. Feel free to take the time you need to think about what could be keeping you on the fence.

Whatever the reason, just know that going to therapy doesn't mean you're broken. Get that out of your mind, right now.

For me, my panic attack definitely had me thinking, I wish I had a trusted resource in place before I got to this point. That I had let go any shame of going to therapy before that point and maybe, perhaps maybe, this whole panic attack could have been avoided. *But it is what it is*, I thought. Now had to be the time. I had no idea how to search for a therapist, so naturally I used Google. I turned to Google because, at the time, when I thought about asking my friends for a recommendation for a therapist, I immediately imagined how the sessions would go.

First session: "Hi, I was referred by Referral Friend."

A few sessions later: "You know Referral Friend really pissed me off last week when they did this. Oh wait, can I talk about them here? You're not going to tell them, right?"

The whole referral from a friend just felt like a conflict of interest and a series of uncomfortable situations. So Google it was. I ended up finding my therapist very quickly. I was solving for first my issue (anxiety) and my second (location). I didn't want to drive far in my panicked state. It turned out the church in my neighborhood, which I attended off and on, had a whole therapy practice with licensed therapists. They were faith-based in that they sought to find a holistic way to therapy. I had no idea what that meant, but I was down for it.

Holistic seemed low friction in my mind and, being new to therapy, I knew I didn't want to feel overwhelmed. As it turned out, my first experience in therapy this way delivered what it was supposed to. No grand aha moments, no extreme tears, just discussing my anxiety and finding tools to help me work through it. My therapist was kind and very learning focused. She spoke in a very caring tone and took notes and listened intently. We would talk about something in one session and then, by the next session, she would have a host of worksheets for me to fill out to specifically target that issue.

Who knew therapy could be like school? I thought. My inner overachieving immigrant child was delighted. I aimed to ace therapy. And for a while, I did; I worked through my panic attack episode and even other fears I had that created heavy anxiety for me, like flying. Don't ask me why, but although I had flown hundreds, if not thousands, of times and lived abroad, every plane ride was torture. With my first therapist I was able to really face the fear head on. Not make my anxiety disappear, but acknowledge it and not let it rule my emotions or, even worse, ruin my day.

I call the experience I had in therapy then my paint-by-numbers therapy experience. It was easy, the problem was clear, the steps were even clearer, and there was no need to get super deep. Or rather, I chose not to because even though I'd previously had therapy FOMO, now that I was in therapy to fix what

I deemed the problem (my panic attack), I still didn't want to be labeled a regular therapy-goer. (Again, read: Black girl too proud and embarrassed to say she goes to therapy.) I just needed to finish the painting or, in this case, get in control of my fears by following the steps. And I did it. At some point my therapist and I were comfortable with where I was, and I essentially "graduated" from anxiety and fear-focused therapy. I felt complete, for a while at least.

It wasn't until about a year later, when I was undertaking a big change in my business, that I started remembering my therapy sessions and thinking, *How did I finish therapy?* I mean people are in therapy for years or their entire lifetime, and here I am, done. Something felt incomplete. My FOMO was kicking back in, but even more so, my shame was wearing off. I had enough insight after my first therapy experience to know that it was helpful even if I treaded lightly, and I think that's something that you should know. Treading lightly in therapy is a thing and can be helpful to you if that's the best you can do. I think there's too much pressure put into therapy having to be an all-out crying or resolution session. Even now, and I'm no longer treading lightly in therapy as much, I still have sessions in which not much is being discussed that could be deemed really serious or intense, and they are still useful. Having someone to discuss things with in general makes the light moments feel important.

So back to Google searching I went. I was ready to find a therapist for consistency. This part of my therapy journey is what I call the "I need a therapist that under-stands me because she is just like me" approach.

Transparently, my first therapist was a white woman, so I started to think, *Maybe I finished therapy because she didn't understand the real issues I may be dealing with because she doesn't understand me, a Black woman. I need someone that's going to see me, and know, "Sis, demographically alone, you should be here."* I needed a Black woman therapist. She would know what to do. *She would never graduate me*, I thought. She would stick around and support me because she knows that something could always come up in the life of a Black woman. I may or may not have been right about that, but looking back, I probably wasn't really open enough with my first therapist to even express that there could be other things I needed to discuss and that I was looking for an ongoing therapist relationship. Coming off a type-A fueled panic attack, I went into my first thera-pist experience on a type-A like mission.

But this time, location didn't matter. As long as she was licensed in my state, which are the guidelines for therapy and counseling practices, we could make it work. I was more open to telehealth anyways, given my schedule. Plus, with the crazy changes that were going on in my business, which is what prompted me to even have the thoughts to seek out a therapist that could be a relatable confidant, telehealth would probably be more ideal.

I typed in "Black woman therapist Florida." Pages upon pages appeared in my search. Once again, Google nailed it. I read through bio after bio, looking for someone I thought could offer not only a listening ear that was understanding to who I was as a Black woman, but someone who was also well versed in dealing with Black women professionals looking to take their career, or in my case business, to the next level.

After going back and forth on my search results for a few days, I found her. She was based out of New York and Florida, where I lived, and not only was she a licensed mental health counselor, she was also a business performance coach. She had a prework questionnaire, light work for me since I was already used to workbook-style therapy, and then we were all set to schedule our first appointment. I was anxious in a good way. It felt great, like I accomplished something. I couldn't wait to talk to who would be my therapy match. Finding a therapist was indeed very much like dating, and the criteria I was looking for seemed to be met: location, availability, cultural likeness.

What was most important was the last thing, cultural likeness. We needed to be aligned on certain things and I had decided that this was definitely it. This part, to this day, I have not waivered on. And although I can see how it may be limiting, and maybe I could find a therapist match with someone completely outside of my culture, I've had success in where I've landed today given my comfort level around our cultural fit. And that is the greater takeaway: you have to prioritize what makes you the most comfortable when choosing a therapist. And that I do.

The day of our first session with my new BGIRL

therapist finally rolled around. In our email corre-
spondences, we decided ahead of time that we would
plan virtual sessions, and that would be our primary
way of meeting, but we always had the option to
change to an in-person session on the days she was
actually in the Florida office near where I lived. I was
on time and logged on ready to divulge everything
about me so she could get to work and guide me to
the next big moment of clarity I needed—how to jug-
gle everything, and how to do it well. As soon as I got
there, she was already on. Major plus for me. Nothing I hated more than waiting at the doctor's office,
or in this case, the virtual therapist office. Her face
was smiley and welcoming. *Good for her*, I thought,
it couldn't be me.

She welcomed me and let me know she read
through all the prework I sent over and was looking
forward to serving me as my therapist but she had a
question first that she needed to clarify. My incon-
sistent smiley face ceased immediately and my eyes
nearly rolled. What question could she have? Maybe
it was about the prework. I thought I'd answered the
questions pretty clearly. It didn't seem like anything
would need clarification.

But then she asked: "Aren't you [one my BFFs of
twenty years]'s friend? You don't remember me? We
met when you came up to New York and we all went
out."

I was floored.

WTF? I screamed inside. All my days of Google searching and vetting, and my blind party days

had caught up with me. Not only did I not recognize her, I vaguely, maybe, maybe not, I really wasn't sure, remembered her. She went on to provide details of when we met, how she knew me, and to confirm yes, she was the friend of one of my BFF's sisters. I was on an indefinite pause and couldn't speak. I was shocked and she could tell. So she went on to say that we'd only met once, yes, but she did feel like she should tell me because, under some therapy rule, she was required to let me know. It was my decision if I wanted to continue to move forward. She stressed how our sessions would remain confidential and that my comfort was the number one priority.

I listened and then stopped listening. I couldn't come to grips that, after all my Google searching and research, a simple Facebook friends search would have avoided this. We weren't friends on Facebook, but if I had seen one mutual friend at any time before this, I would have never moved forward. My biggest therapy fear was not therapy itself. It was going to a therapist who knew me. To me, the biggest plus about therapy is that it is supposed to be a neutral third party. And to that end, the biggest catastrophe would be if it were someone who knew me and the people I knew. There would be no neutrality, no confidence that this information was truly confidential. I didn't know what to do. My comfort level immediately dropped.

Well of course, the part of me that is overwhelmingly let's-just-finish-what-I-started made the decision. I eventually gathered enough confidence and told her we should move forward and that if at any point in time I felt uncomfortable, we would just stop the sessions. I also decided we would only engage in the business coaching side of her practice, and we could specifically focus on the tools I needed to get through the current challenge I was facing. Once that was accomplished, I again would "graduate."

All in all, it was not really what I was looking for going into this round of therapy. I was looking for a fellow Black girl confidant and didn't want to graduate therapy again, but it worked for what I immediately needed. I was dealing with stressors related to my business and I wanted a Black woman therapist who had some context to that experience. What I can tell you is that it confirmed that finding the right therapist can be difficult. It's not always a one-shot thing, and sometimes, just like it's OK to tread lightly, it is also OK to do the work with a therapist who is not a complete fit but will be helpful to you to realign and think through what is a better fit.

After I got through my set amount of sessions with this second therapist, I knew I would be back at it again. I was frustrated but, at the same time, understood this is how it was going to be. I was going to once again "graduate"—this time by choice—and be on my search again. At least I now confirmed that I would be putting in the work and staying consistent. No more graduations, at least not so early in the journey.

With my second therapist, I kept it highly professional and high level, but my confidence in our sessions remaining confidential just never was there. I never told her this because I felt like it would be going back on my original commitment to get through the business challenge, but I'm sure she sensed it. I did make it to the end of all our sessions though, and I did work through the business challenges I was having. We set goals around the confidence I was having at executing the goals and even now I would consider again having a therapist who focuses on the specific nuances of being in leadership or running your own company. It was extremely helpful, and while I may not have gotten a confidant out of it, I did get an accountability partner for the time that we did work together. What I didn't do was start seeking out the next therapist at the same time. Similar to dating, I am a one relationship at a time girl. It also felt like it would be exhausting to have to be emotionally vulnerable with two people simultaneously.

When I was in the clear and had some distance from the experience with the second therapist, I started my search again. At that point, I felt the most emotionally secure I'd felt in a long while; there was no panic attack on the horizon and my business and career stressors were manageable This phase of the search was now pointed, a culmination of the two experiences before. I knew I wanted consistency, cultural likeness, and now, anonymity. I did not need to be seeing my therapist out on these streets and vice versa. This time I put my social media skills to work and made sure I cross-referenced every Black girl IRL therapist I came across that could be a fit. Did you attend the same undergrad or grad school that I did? Nope, not going to work. The Black communities are too small in those places, and I don't care if we didn't attend at the same time. Lived in the same city I currently lived in? Also a no. Even part-time living here isn't going to work. I wasn't going to risk it as evident by my last therapist who flew back and forth.

Besides getting all of the other criteria out of the way in regards to type of therapy fit, my biggest aha moment was during the break when I didn't have a therapist. The support I was looking for was a true advocate. I aced my criteria again, but I ran into a personality mismatch with my third therapist. I said therapy and finding a therapist was like dating and I mean it. Personalities matter. Again, like dating, so many things can be right on paper but then when you're together in person, something is just not right. I'm blunt and have a healthy level of optimism with a balance of pessimism. My new therapist, though, turned out to be the Wednesday Addams of Black girl therapy. At least that's how she came across to me.

When I logged into our first virtual therapy session there was no smiling face looking back at me. I mean, it wasn't required but sure would have felt nice given I felt hopeful and happy about where things were in my life and had mentioned in the prequestionnaire (she had one too) that exact feeling. I also mentioned I was seeking out therapy as just an added benefit in life. But what made things worse and what really threw me off was that talking to her, or rather her talking to me, was like listening to a Black Daria.

Love Daria, but not for therapy. I had to remind myself during the session to keep it together to get through it. Her voice was monotone and had the same enthusiasm she had on her face—none. There's no way this was the advocate therapist I was looking for. For me, it wasn't going to work. Even if my life would eventually reflect the doomsday vibes she was giving me, I would need someone who at least gave off some light at the end of the tunnel, and sis was not it. I decided I would respectfully continue the whole initial session but there would be no sessions after that.

Here's where I say it sucks. Just as I stuck with getting through that session, I had to once again stick through the commitment of finding a therapist, and you may have to as well. If trusting the process means one, two, or even three therapists to get to the right one, you have to keep on going. If we, as Black women, don't give up on our goals, we shouldn't give up on this either, especially if it feels like we'll never find our fit. The investment in therapy is for our health, our mental health. It's for the good times and the bad times. It's how we become better advocates for ourselves and how we manage all that comes our way. It's how we take care of ourselves.

While therapist number three at this point was an epic fail from a personality perspective, I learned that box-checking wasn't going to be my only screener. The therapist trait of feeling like an advocate for me had to be expressed in the way we interacted. Tone, personality, resting facial expressions, all of that mattered. Again, like dating, have your criteria and know it going into the search and, for that matter, your first few sessions.

I decided I'd need to tell my next therapist up front that I'm searching for a fit and that I'd like our initial session to be us seeing if we work together well. I felt more confident going into the session with therapist number four some weeks later. I filled out the prework—at this point, I'm an advocate for someone creating a system that has a universal prework question database for therapy, so I don't have to answer variations on the same questions over and over again, but that's for another time—and I sent it back via email. When I scheduled a session, she graciously reached out to me via text. I had learned from therapist number three that I like a therapist that texts, so at least something good came out of it. With number four, she asked if I'd like to move my therapy session up because she had an opening that was earlier than the more than six weeks out I had scheduled. I accepted the earlier sessions, and then we were good to go.

To say I scored with my fourth and now current therapist would be an understatement. But then again, I went through three before her so it wasn't happenstance, it was putting in the work. I had criteria, I had sessions with other therapist, I filled out a bunch of prework and questionnaires, and stuck through some uncomfortable situations. Just like we Black girls do for so many other things, for this I had to as well. My current therapist is Black, on time, sends text messages, does virtual sessions, coached high performance women, is a mom of little ones, and truly listens with an understanding ear. Did I mention that she smiles and has various tones when speaking?

My current therapist is what I need for the now part of my life. And that's how I explain it to people. I don't know how long it will last or if she would have worked for other parts of my life, but she works great now. She's not only a confidant, she's also a supporter. She pushes me to discuss my accomplishments and not shy away from them, and she provides the supportive language that doesn't come easy for me to tell myself. There's been not so great moments we've discussed too. She has seen the internal grief I've experienced and has been able to help me feel it but then continue on. For me at this moment I need a therapist who sees my life in an overall positive light. It's not that the others didn't, but I needed someone who expresses that to me blatantly and helps me internalize that feeling as well. Call it my "therapist love language" I suppose. She gets me and I'd like to think that our sessions feel fulfilling for her therapy practice as well.

The journey to a great therapist can be exactly that, a journey. You may find the perfect match on your first go or you may settle for some time or you may experience some hard no, do not proceed moments. In a lot of ways, the search for a therapist can mirror the search for a partner. After all, your relationship with your therapist is extremely personal. It involves developing a level of trust to share your innermost thoughts and feelings with someone else.

For me, I really had no idea going into finding a therapist that it would be a multiyear process, but telling myself upfront that I was going to commit to finding one is what got me to continue. Therapy FOMO and then my panic attack induced a must-find-a-therapist mode but also made me evaluate what my prior hesitance had been. I also could really evaluate what I desired from therapy.

Questions to ask yourself that may be helpful to use in the process of finding your ideal therapist could be: Who do I want to share my story with? Is there something that signals to me that someone is a safe space to do so? What is it? Have I taken note of this? Also, what are my nonnegotiables? Are there things that I know going into the process that won't work for me? And most important, what am I looking to achieve in therapy? Is there something pressing I want to resolve? Or is therapy just part of my overall wellness plan right now? Both are perfectly good reasons, by the way.

These days, most of my friends are in or have been through some type of therapy. It's interesting to hear their therapy wins. It feels less like we are talking about a taboo subject or something that we should be ashamed of. That, in itself, feels good. Even more encouraging is that more and more Black women are making the time for therapy. We got a lot going on, sis. Having a listening ear is sometimes all we need to decompress the life of a Black girl IRL. Therapy may be that wellness bump you need. When I moved past that first urgent phase, I landed where I wished I was already when I got started. Therapy became a tool in my self-improvement box that is consistently accessible to me.

I hope you too get to experience that consistency.

Truth #7

Social Media (and the Internet) Is the Real MVP

I've been to college twice, undergrad and grad school. Two degrees, one in economics and an MBA, and neither of those degrees taught me as much as I've learned from as a result of social media. Facts. The way I've been able to pursue what I'm passionate about, interact with people who share similar interests, and really up my overall life game has been unmatched.

Case in point, in undergrad, I went deep into studying health-care economics and infrastructure. I took courses on patient outcomes and pricing within health-care systems. I thought I was about to revolutionize the health-care system. Four years of those classes, and the hold times every time I try to call my insurance company to find out why they didn't cover something at a doctor's visit takes me out. I've gotten more benefit from the breathing exercises I've googled while waiting on these calls to calm my nerves than whatever I learned about health-care billing and pricing. At the end of the day, I just want to speak to an actual person faster and I find myself looking up "How to reach a person at—?" and "What option to press to reach a person at—?" more often these days. That's what the internet does, gets me straight to the answers. There are even TikToks and YouTube videos on how to reach a customer service agent. People already know someone else will find this information useful.

I question the full utility of my education when I look back at grad school similarly. I dove deep into quantitative analysis and took tons of courses on financial modeling and valuation. In my second year I doubled down on marketing research and statistics. In my mind I would become the marketing expert of experts. So when I opened my first business, I put all that financial and marketing training to work. I had projections on projections based on an extensive marketing plan to get customers, it was planned out to the T. Then within weeks Instagram did one of its many changes to their algorithm. And yeah, that was a fail. You know the deal. Our posts stopped showing up as often in the news feed and engagement dropped. Those spreadsheets predicting total market takeover meant nothing. Six years of higher education, and all I needed to do was follow what the latest influencer trends were for engaging with followers and take note. Time to do that? A couple of hours.

This isn't a knock on higher education. It definitely served a purpose. The people I met, the launching of my career, the places I was able to live, invaluable. But today, I can tell you for a fact that the world changes faster than the curriculum that schools and printed books can keep up with. If I need to reduce my hold time or build a brand that's more influential, I'm finding the answer to that online. Social media and the internet are always up to date. Plus, with the amount of experts present on these platforms, fact checking becomes easier—and of course is an always necessary step. With that in place I'm rarely led astray. Once we embrace that education and life changing improvements can and are facilitated by social media and what is found online, Black girls, we are unstoppable.

We've got to get comfortable that social media's primary purpose is to be a means to further improve our lives. We have to stop all that *mindless* scrolling. Online resources are often so lush, most of the time, it's the first place I check if I want to get an idea about something. New business idea? I'm googling similar businesses and checking their Instagram and social pages to see who follows them and what they are saying. Saw a hairstyle on my favorite celebrity and I want to get an idea of how it's going to look on me and who can get it done? I'm searching hashtags on Instagram and stylists on StyleSeat. "Black girl with bob," "medium knotless braids," "Senegalese twists," all searches my web browser sees on a regular.

What's great about social media that I didn't get from my school education is the diversity factor. It's right there on the platform and in your face. The way Black women show up, show out, and let it be known that we are in that industry, have that hobby, or are partaking in that leisure activity, it is so amazing! It gives me the confidence to jump right in too and get acquainted with whatever it is. Some of the most influential accounts I follow make me want to be and do better. It's like their content screams, "Oh, are you thinking about joining too, girl? Come on over, there's room for you here too," with none of that awkward, "Am I the only Black person in this room?" feeling.

So sure, some people are using social media to practice their auditions for their next potential music video or uploading TikTok dance videos (no shade, I just don't have that level of confidence yet), but because of this "come join us" environment you can find your stride in networking and getting to know more people that have similar interests that you couldn't just stumble upon outside. I don't know about you but I'm a visual learner, so the overactive internet that screams "watch me do it first, then you try" is my happy place. I can join groups of interests, DM and chat with people who are not in my city, and get ideas and tips on new things I want to try out. With social media, I see it, I learn it, I can try it, and even get immediate feedback on it if that's what I want. Even better, everything is at my own pace. There's no due date and no grades, and best of all, no expectations but my own. If someone asks me how I use social media? It's simple. I've curated a place that's full of all the Black girl influence and personal growth that I love.

In short, social media is the game changer that you need. Look past the background of idle updates about people's lives that you wouldn't have followed in real life in the first place, and focus on your next hustle, your next Black mom group, or your next entrepreneur circle sharing their firsthand knowledge. Me personally, I am following the accounts of women who look like me, Black women who are putting out high quality content that boasts excellence. Let me tell you, that excellence? Whew! Black women really have been owning social media and the internet. Yes, you everyday Black woman who felt the need to educate your fellow Black queens on the latest hacks from style, beauty, fashion, and health so that we can continue looking and doing our best. You are and have been the crux of that social media and internet come up I'm talking about.

In the past five years, having gone from dating and unmarried to married with two kids, life has been coming at me more than fast. Time seems even more limited than before. My life needs to be efficient, and sometimes I don't have the time to do things the long way like I used to when it was just me, myself, and I. I need a shortcut for everything. The number one thing that changed for me was hair care.

I used to love a good sew in (and still do!), but the time that requires for me to be in the chair at the salon is not always available. Plus, in this mom lifestyle, I'm unreliable. One minute I could be headed to the beauty salon and the next minute I'm making a U-turn because my kid has a fever and he's being sent home. Trust me, it's happened before. And I know it's just a season of life I'm living now, where managing two toddlers doesn't give me eight hours several times a month to be in a salon and indulge in hair care self-care, but for now I needed a solution. And thanks to you, the fabulous Black women of the internet, I've been able to actually embrace my natural hair. I always did and always do love my natural hair, but I really stepped up my ability to manage my natural hair without it being a time-consuming event thanks to all the tips and tricks I've found.

From natural hair care products to protective styles, I can pull up a video online on any platform to get ideas and inspiration for the week, whether I want to keep it super low maintenance or find something fancy for an event. Sometimes I surprise myself with how good I've gotten at my home hair care routine but then again why should I be? When Black women come through, we really do big time. Ever watched a product review or tutorial done by a Black woman? Superior. HSN and QVC need to take note. Never will they lead you astray. No following ridiculous suggestions to use a "dollop" when we know well and good we need about half the bottle to cover our mane. And the number of times my coils really came through after following the advice of one of these wonderful Black hair vlogger queens on what order to use the products? Countless. Black women take the online video tutorial format by storm every single time. They're not only instructing, they've conducted their own R&D and have perfected what you really need to know.

It doesn't stop at my personal hair care routine.

I've found my people, other Black girls, with similar interests, all over the internet. My Black Girl Magic Peloton group. I love them on and off the internet. They curate rides, meetups, and give tips on any and everything. The women in that group rally behind each other through life events and happenings. Nothing feels forced or awkward. Someone will share a life update or that they hit a goal and you feel honored that you're in the space where that can happen without negativity or animosity. In the same vein I've found several Black moms crews online, all over and locally. Spaces that we as Black mothers can share and grow together. It is so important for Black mothers to have a sounding board and space where there are other moms who understand the cultural and real-life nuances of being a Black mom. They know things like how navigating bullying can be different when you're the mom of a Black child. And they've experienced the subtle eyerolls and "mmhmms" from our moms and aunties who may not like our new way of parenting. Parenting is hard and the Black mom groups I've been able to connect with online and now offline have made it feel like a manageable hard.

You know what else I've become because of social media? Truly more knowledgeable. I take in so much more information because it is actually accessible at my fingertips at any time of the day. Online platforms have increased my desire to read and research. I already follow Black women whom I admire, so I'm always getting behind what they say makes them tick and succeed. If they have a book recommendation,

I'm buying it. If they post an interesting article, I make sure to save it to read later. Interviews, Ted Talks, MasterClasses, or even courses that offer the ability to be in a room with them and absorb some of their skills and expertise—I'm paying for it. In my opinion I've spent thousands on education at schools that in the past I would not have been able to attend because I was a Black woman, so when a Black woman is ready to teach me what she knows, I'm not hesitating to spend money on it. Ten times out of ten it's valuable information just because she is Black. That's not a perspective or experience that I was exposed to with any frequency in formal education.

My inner Black girl smarty-pants self really enjoys learning about everything. I used to be so annoyed when I'd ask my dad how to do something and his first response was "Look it up." Back then looking it up meant going to the library and using the card catalog system or sifting through the *Encyclopedia Britannica* that somehow every household got tricked into buying and was immediately outdated the year you bought them. It was a hassle and I always ended up with more questions than answers. To this day he still says "Look it up" when you ask him about something. And now that he's up in age it comes across exactly as one would expect it to when you hear an older Black man say "Look it up," like half crochety and half guiding light. And my friends, that guiding light should direct us to the internet.

My dad, himself an early adapter to the internet, uses YouTube to basically learn everything that he already doesn't know. Of course, it's usually related to home improvement and cars but he loves it. Things like fixing something with the air conditioning or the roof. And recently he surprised us and stepped into the DIY influencer world himself. He sent a YouTube link to the family group chat. We opened the link and what did we see? My dad, a sixty-five-year-old Black man, had created his own DIY YouTube video. That sharing magic isn't only reserved for us Black girls these days. Never mind that the video was done in true impatient older Black man tempo and it gets to the point very, very quickly, so quickly you almost miss it. He definitely shows you what the problem is—in this case something to do with fixing a toilet bowl, don't ask. And then he rapidly says, "This is how you fix it" while demonstrating how to make the repair, and then the camera stops, abruptly ending the video. My dad has gone from following videos he finds online to getting the confidence to make one himself—guiding all the people also "looking it up" in need of random toilet repair, whoever these people are.

But, sis, let's take a pause. As productive as social media and the internet can be and transformative as the resources available through them are, as with anything, too much of a good thing can become a bad thing. Comparison is the thief of joy and social media can be the window into heavy comparison. Ever login into your social account and it seems like everyone is out on vacation? Then you spend time trying to figure out how it's possible that they have that much time off since they were just on vacation last week? What I said in the beginning about getting caught up spending too much time minding other people's business on social media is a real risk. There are people I've spoken to maybe once or twice in real life and have immediately gone on to add me as their "friend" in social media. Remember what I said about not answering every call in life? Well sometimes that friend request is that call that doesn't need to be answered. On its face there should really be no problem accepting friend requests and connecting with people you've just met. But I'm always wary of what people see and think who don't really know me or that I don't really know. How much of what is posted is a true reflection of what's going on? What conclusions are being drawn about my life or theirs? The context is not there. The call to leave out the social part of social media at times, when it feels like it could be counterproductive, is an OK one to make, sis.

I for one used to get so caught up in what I would call the not useful parts of social media, whether it be people or brands I followed that weren't serving me. Instead of getting inspiration, guidance, or new ideas, I was getting body image issues and the feeling of not doing enough. I was trying to keep up with the life and look I thought I needed to have. My number one disclaimer I have for using social media and online spaces to enhance and optimize your fabulous Black girl life is to unfollow, mute, detach, and put away whatever doesn't serve you the minute it doesn't serve you. Your feelings start shifting from inspired to competitive or even left behind when you login? Evaluate and unfollow what doesn't work for you. Spending more time drawing inspiration and less time doing and taking action in real life? Take a break. Social media needs to be controlled.

Not too long ago I read a book called *Digital Minimalism* by Cal Newport. It was so helpful in putting healthy boundaries around the digital world in general. It touches on so many great points but for me the most applicable one is deciding how I am going to interact with the digital world. And although I proclaim my love for social media in an ode to how great it has been to simplify my life, I spend less time on it than most people. What works for me is fifteen minutes a day. In fifteen minutes I can get in and get out without getting distracted by what's not serving me in the process. I know that for me anything more than fifteen minutes becomes idle scrolling. How else do I control my usage? On a platform with people "I know," meaning all the friends I've accepted requests from, I mute all notifications and updates about them on my feed. The information I need to know, from the people I need to know it from, will be communicated directly to me via phone, email, text, or in person because they have sought out to tell me and vice versa. Intentional communication is how we are wired to receive most information, not from browsing for hours. This also forces me to intentionally keep in touch and have relationships with the people I want to maintain this type of connection with, which if I'm speaking honestly is not with the hundreds of people on my friend list.

Remember back in the day when your mom would drop you off at the mall to meet up with your friends? With no cell phones, everyone was able to determine the meetup location and time and magically also get picked up, albeit there was always someone who was the last to get picked up. Some kids (ahem, not me) were even slick enough to get dropped off at one location, go with their friends to another location they were not supposed to be at, and make it right back to the drop-off location in time for pick up. All of this happened without the constant communication and checking in via cell phones. That's how I feel about social media feeds. I'm not sure our brains were designed to watch over one hundred people at any given time document their entire morning routine down to the outfits they were choosing between and the traffic they were sitting in. When I intentionally mute everyone I am friends with on social media I am also intentionally opening up the doors of communication in real life to the people I really do know or have a desire to get to know better.

The gist of it all this is: use social media to your advantage not to your disadvantage. If in any way it begins to feel overwhelming or harmful, stop. There's nothing there that won't be there tomorrow. A habit I started to intentionally calibrate is taking digital sabbaticals. It still feels kind of scary every time I do it, like what am I missing out on? What's going on that I'm missing? But a few days in, those feelings completely disappear because I actually enjoy talking to the people in my house in an uninterrupted way and sleeping without hearing my phone vibrate. And when I do return to the digital world, I am aligned to doing so intentionally. Recently, I've even gone as far as deleting all social media apps from my phone, so when I do catch up, it's in an intentional setting at my desk and not just because I'm bored waiting in line somewhere. It helps me prioritize the people around me. You know what further pushed me to delete all my apps and create a fixed location to scroll social media? My son, who was three years old at the time.

It only took him screaming "Mommy, get off your phone!" one time while we were doing the dreaded waiting in line, and that was it, I was off. If my three-year-old could recognize that my attention in the moment was just not there, I immediately knew that for me it just wasn't necessary to have that type of distraction at my fingertips. Besides, wasn't time alone with him doing nothing enough? No need to fill every minute of the day with doing. We already have enough to do.

Social media should be flexible in how you use it but ultimately give you leverage where you need it. Because Black women, we deserve leverage. Whether it be our finances, our relationships, or our skill set, social media should be a tool. It is a useful space where we can commune with each other as we share ways to up our game and not have to build the life we want all alone. It might sound trivial, but things like getting my time back after I found the hair styling looks that work for me, which in the past were so time consuming, and being able to show up looking and feeling my best, is an instant confident booster for me. And when you're confident, you're unstoppable. Things like keeping up with an exercise routine, because being healthy is important so that I can keep showing up for my family, is made easier with my online community of other Black women who know the specific demands that only we have. Social media, the MVP, the GOAT, and all that great stuff is a tool. But it's a means to an end. Never the full picture but a useful part of the picture. Staying focused and intentional keeps it in the place of positively impacting our lives, and immediately eliminating the parts that don't work for us reiterates its purpose.

Truth #8

Black People Own Pelotons Too . . . and Other Assumed White Lifestyle Items

Black women and Black girls are the flyest group of people I know. We are everything. We carry the direction of whole industries just by our influence. So much is created and curated off what we've introduced into this world. We set the pace for what's coming next. Not only is our influence necessary, without it, many companies would be in dire straits if we weren't the consumers of influence that we are. Our choices make or break the financial future of the world.

The beauty industry, for example, has expanded by billions of dollars just from being more inclusive to Black women and our features, or products that are meant to emulate our features. Within the fitness industry, the high-energy, music-based workouts that have made their way into everything from cycling to running are created with the rhythm and soul of Black culture. Put plainly, life for everyone would be pretty boring if we weren't here. We are the cake and the icing on top.

Whatever Goop, Poosh, or the latest double vowel brand's following tells you is trending, you can just go ahead and throw that out. Black women will tell you what's on trend and what's not, if it's worth it, or what's the next best thing. They will spare no details and even tell you how you can get it for the low, if available. Black women are the original Yelp, Angie's List, and Trip Advisor, and have feelings about everything. So, when it comes to products, places, and things in general, we waste no time developing an opinion.

That's why when I tell people I'm in a social group for Black women Peloton owners, I'm always surprised when they seem shocked. Usually their first response is "Really?" or some version of "Wow, that's interesting." Then they start asking me a ton of questions about the group like they're getting insight into some lost civilization. I'm not sure if their reaction is because there is a group like this that exists, or because I, a Black woman, own a Peloton, or the combination of the two. Either way, yes: Black women own Pelotons, and they have their own social group about this shared interest.

A Black woman owning a Peloton is an item on the long list of things, interests, activities, you name it that other people continue to be shocked to learn about us. It is as if, despite the fact that we are a functioning part of society—and I'd venture to say *the* functioning part of society—Black women still aren't supposed to have and enjoy the things that other people enjoy in their lives. It's like we shouldn't have gotten the memo that life should be enjoyable, and people are shocked when they find out we did. It always comes across as a news flash for everyone but us when Black women have the "audacity" to show up in an area of life they didn't expect us to be. So I'm here to say, keep showing up on that Peloton leaderboard, sis, keep showing up.

Most people really don't know who we are. Black women are the original "been there done that" and "I'll take one of everything" girls. We work hard, play hard, and always know what's up, despite whatever your local news segments may be "discovering." We've been interested in everything and we've been doing everything. They have no idea who Black women really are.

Where I saw this bias about what was for Black people and specifically me, a Black girl, show up early on was about music. Despite the immense influence, from the creation of genres to the masterminding and dominance of the charts, across all genres, Black people are continually typecast into the musical genres that are "our" music: hip-hop and R&B. Now look, hip-hop and R&B *are* our music, we are good at it and the sounds and rhymes we produce are genius, but that doesn't mean we don't listen to other types of music.

When I was in fifth grade, a classmate's dad was associated with the band Green Day. She gave us T-shirts and a CD from her dad's connections. I'd never listened to Green Day before that, and as a fifth grader I was barely into the music scene; I also wasn't really aware they were a white band. But as soon as I went home and put that Green Day CD into my boombox, that was it, it was instant, I loved Green Day. My favorite song on the album, "Basket Case," played over and over again. I restarted the opening line at least a hundred times. *Do you have the time to listen to me whine?* Yes, Green Day, I absolutely did. I loved everything about them—the vocals, the guitar, the vocals over the guitar. It just sounded good, and what Black people like is good music. That's really just it.

A few weeks after I got that Green Day album, I wanted more. I went to the music store at the mall and went through the rock section. I was determined to find more bands that I liked like Green Day. That's how I found the Cranberries, and I was geeked to find them. There was something melodically hypnotic about their songs, especially "Zombie." I loved that I'd found this music to add to all the other types of music I was already listening to.

This was part of who I was growing up as a Black girl with mostly Black close friends. My friends and I would discover new things, regardless of who they were assumed to be intended for, and we couldn't wait to share it with each other any time we met up. We were singing "Zombie! Zombie! Zombieee!" and also trying to keep pace with the opening verse of every hip-hop song—"Now, who's hot, who's not? Tell me who rock, who sell out in the stores?" Years later and I'm still doing the same thing. In college, it was Lil Jon or Coldplay, and I was going to sing my songs, and now it's my H.E.R., Beyoncé, SZA, Taylor Swift, and Imagine Dragons. I'm still singing my songs, whatever the genre is.

But even though I had friends when I was growing up who I could relate to and vibe with across genres of music and things that we just liked that were not considered "Black," that doesn't mean it came without criticism and chatter from my own people. I remember for a good part of elementary and middle school, my friends and I were called Oreos by some of the other Black kids. We were Black on the outside and white on the inside, just like Oreo cookies, according to them. It didn't matter that my obvious dark brown skin, Black girl hair and hairstyles, and all of my other physical traits indicated clearly that I was Black.

To some of my classmates, I was just not Black enough.

That's when I had the realization at an early age that, even among Black people, there wasn't a universal acceptance of each other. Not only was I learning that people outside our race didn't think I fit in, but inside my race some of the same feelings came to the surface. Outside of my race, it felt like I had to prove it was OK for me to step out of the bounds of what was expected of Blackness. And inside my race, among my own Black people, I felt like I had to prove that I was indeed Black enough to be one of us.

In adulthood, it became less of a factor because I really know who I am. I know that my choice in music, art, TV, or even how I speak doesn't determine my race and ethnicity or whether I should be accepted. The thing is though that while you are a kid still fig- uring out who you are and trying new things, it can feel very isolating, even when you are part of the group of Oreos like I was. It wasn't only me and my friends struggling to figure out where we fit in among Black people. Many of us Black girls IRL were also looking for our place and, in some cases, still are. I was lucky to have a group of friends that shared in my interests, but what happens when you don't? When you know what you like and enjoy but you can't find a common place among any of your people? We have to learn how to stand strong and be comfortable in and about ourselves, regardless of the messaging, the jabs, or the shade. This isn't a route that is by any means easy, but it's the route that will help you feel and remain the most true, the most authentic, and the most whole version of yourself.

And, ladies, we *gotta* be there for each and every one of us trying to find our accepting community, whether we understand someone's likes or not. That's not for us to pass judgment on. Point blank, period.

Whether its in the workplace, within our fami- lies, or in our Black girl friend group, when there's an idea that dominates what it means to be Black, it is limiting not only to others but also to yourself if you no longer fit that ideal. I am still into pop culture and music. I still like some alternative rock, and I also read my horoscope at times. I enjoy those things and I also enjoy being Black. These two things can be true at once. Admittedly, my likes aren't the most extreme that fall outside of many people's "what it is to be Black" box but what about those of us Black girls who like things that overwhelmingly skew more toward non-Black culture? There's a whole movement of Black girls who are anime and manga aficionados, and others who relate to goth subculture and aesthetic. For them, judgment and criticism from our own folk may come more quickly and feel harsher, as those interests are not necessarily dominant in Western culture either. But that is who they are authentically and who they should be allowed to be.

I've observed that what is considered "Black enough" is held with more rigidity in older generations. The influence of that trickles down. How we address and speak about Blackness in front of young kids is powerful. I don't believe that kids just came up with calling another kid an Oreo back in grade school on their own. Black children, children in general, are not born with an approval meter on what constitutes the right way to dress, the right music to listen to, or even the right religion to have. These things are all taught and observed and then adapted. Some things we adapt by choice, others by habit. Since we are no longer children, we have the opportunity as Black women to do the work of accepting everyone, especially our fellow Black girls, regardless of how they present themselves to the world. Acceptance for us means that the things that constitute being Black are a spectrum and even if it's not *our* thing, we can be respectful when other people show up as their true selves.

Being in community with other Black women, I know that other Black girls may still be hurt or even resentful of the sisterhood because of how they were judged previously when they showed up as their authentic selves—when they already were managing anti-Black racism, and then had to take on extra battles of fitting in with the very group they are supposed to belong to. It sucks having to choose authenticity knowing that generational rifts are already more than likely on the menu; a rift among your peers makes it even more burdensome.

Black people and, more specifically Black girls, are a whole spectrum of likes, dislikes, and awesomeness. We don't need to decide for each other how we should show up and shine. If we are going to encourage each other to be our authentic Black girl selves, then that encouragement can't come with a clause. It can't come with a "I'm supportive of you, sis, but only if . . ." We know that any acceptance that comes with a caveat can easily begin to look like the historic ways we as a people have been limited. The support of other Black women, the support of each other from the inside, is the safety blanket we need to maintain for each other. It's the allowance we should give each other because we know other people won't.

And that's the thing with Black culture: it's very distinct and at the same time whatever you want it to be. The Black women I know are "culturally" Black, whatever that means, and not at the same time. In recent times, people may have called it code switching. I understand the intentions around naming the way Black people can move seamlessly in and out of interactions, but I think of it as more of a way for people to define what is actually very natural for us. Black women in particular have masterfully been doing this, always. Case in point: Michelle Obama, First Lady of the White House, attorney, mother, advocate for healthy activities, and consistently going high when they go low. So take note Black women: like what you like and do what you do across everything. Whether it's what expected of you or not, you thrive in those situations.

A phenomenon that happens when Black people show up in spaces other people are surprised we are in is what I call the "Black shock effect." The Black shock effect is a range of reactions by non-Black people. It goes from curious discovery, to ecstatic, to judgmental, to ready to launch an investigation on where to find these Black people with these habits we didn't know about before, and how did they find out about what we are doing. It's an experience just watching it happen.

Ever seen someone's face when they meet you in person and don't expect you to be Black? Your name or voice may not have given them the signal they were waiting for? It happens to me all the time; it's shock. Also ever experience their shock when they realize you know what you're talking about when it comes to something professional, or business related? Priceless. Apparently, no number of years of Black women showing up and showing out can reduce the level of shock experienced. I say to that: keep shocking them,

Black girls. And to take it one step further: shock them in making sure we unapologetically show up to the same table as they do, with our culture engrained in us and on full display as well. What do I mean? I'll tell you.

About every Black woman I know who is invested in wealth building, every one of them has a plan for the dollars that they bring in. The legacy and wealth that we as Black women are setting up to leave behind, whew! It's about to knock down so many systematic biases. When venture capitalist firms or other investment funds don't actively seek us out and support our ideas, we create our own. I've never seen a group of people more determined to fuel our own inclusion and leveling up than Black women. We are investing in other women, creating conferences, teaching and sharing to put us all on. It has become the norm. The resources we share with one another and the openness to do so are abundant and the way knowledge of these things comes into my life is in every area. That's how I know it's here to stay.

As a group we are all on it. But what about things and activities we've kept in the culture? We owe it to ourselves to make sure we let other people recognize how our industries are important to fueling not only us but the economy. To this I say: Black girls run businesses too, and more important, have been running businesses from before we were even allowed to legally participate in the business world.

Take for example Sam, the young lady who braids my hair. She has been braiding hair since she was in high school and got her cosmetology license as soon as she could get one. By the time she was in her junior year of high school, she had a roster of clients. She knew she was really good at braiding. When it was time to graduate, she got a full scholarship to pursue accounting in college, since as she told me, she "really liked numbers." But she still was braiding hair on the side, because that's what she loves to do. Today, Sam runs a braiding business. She still has to validate herself as not "just some hair braider," as she told me. Sam's commitment to hair braiding is more than felt when she talks to you, it is understood. This is her career.

Black women, what you choose to do and how you choose to professionalize it is your career, and it should not be based on a standard of what is thought to be a career and what is not. And because Black women like Sam—and there are plenty—are important as they are. Sam sees clients six days a week, and she also creates a curriculum for the local vocational high school to include braiding in their aesthetician program. Her hope is to have the curriculum expand into other programs so more Black women feel validated that hair braiding is a career and have the training to make it theirs. Sam and Black women like her are sitting at the table, showing up with the businesses that are ours, and making sure they are counted as part of the mainstream business world.

The older I get, the more important it gets for me to dig my heels into owning the things I like, whether other people like it or not. Being a Black woman isn't a predefined box. If I see something that resonates with me, it's for me. Similarly, my culture and the things that represent my culture belong in the mainstream. It's crazy that there has to be legislation (see the Crown Act) to deter people from being outright discriminatory about how we look and style ourselves. One day I may have in a silky straight sew in and the next day I may have my natural 4C coils out. I may talk one way with one person and another way with you—all of that is me. Everything fits into the idea of who I am, a Black woman.

The same goes for you, Black girl: if you like it, it's for you. I've had to get back to the curiosity and propensity to do what I liked when I was younger and lead with that. We spend a lot of years being told what is for us and what's not. The more you get engrained into the "real world," the more things are dictated and assumed about what's really for you. I watch my children now; sure they love the things from our culture that we introduce to them, but they have a genuine unbiased interest in everything. Can you imagine how much could be achieved if we let our own internal judgment take a back seat? And what about when we let the judgment of others also join in that back seat and lead with what we like and really want to do?

The idea that Black people own Pelotons is *meant* to sound obvious and ridiculous. Because of course Black people own Pelotons! The probability that at least one Black person doesn't have something that has been sold to millions is basically improbable. But the idea that Black people, and more particularly

Black women, show up and show out in so many spaces still seems hard to grasp by many people, and sometimes even us, for that matter. What I want is for people's shock about Black women to shift its way into purposeful inclusion and for us to just go ahead and include ourselves on our own. We have to take our own initiative.

How do we do this? Our means. No, I'm not asking you Black women to take on any more jobs, tasks, or chores that will take even more time away from ourselves. But what I do know is that if you spend time in the room with any group of Black people, I don't care what their income is or what they do for a living, and you are going to hear the phrase "generational wealth" or some version of "I'm just trying to take it to the next level." We not only have the means, we are growing our means, and we are also making sure the next generation is better set up than we are. And what is also not so surprising is that while people may deny this as part of our everyday reality, the big companies and financial institutions are beginning to recognize this to be true. Just take a look at the amount of research and spending that goes into trying to see what Black women in particular have interest in and how they can target our interest.

Let us use those generational wealth tools to build and invest in the areas that Black women are showing up in, whether they be culturally affirming areas or things that are assumed for the masses. That's how we become even more powerful in those areas. Think generational wealth is just money? It's not. It's also information. Someone put you on to a new trend that helps improve your life or happiness? Share it with your sis. At a local meetup of enthusiasts you are part of and there's not a lot of faces that look like us in the group but you know people who stan the same thing? Invite them next time. So much of our growth, whether it be financial or experiential, has come from the invitations and inclusion of other Black women. Be the hand that lifts people up.

You don't have to ask me twice about showing up in community for my fellow Black girls. Whether it's joining my all–Black girl magic Peloton group or supporting the businesses that have been engrained in my culture, it's a resounding *yes* from me, and something I look forward to. And you know what? You'll more than likely find me singing Mary J. Blige's "Not Gon' Cry" deep in my soul, followed by Celine Dion's "It's All Coming Back to Me Now," followed by Cardi B's "Bodak Yellow" at karaoke with my girlfriends, because every one of those songs is our song. Just like everything is our thing. Lean into all those yes "Black people do that too" moments. It's a joyous expression of who we are.

Truth #9

Maybe Our Parents Need Reparenting, and Maybe We Do Too

Jesus, Mother Teresa, the Virgin Mary, my mother—all great people who have lived a life without sin. I say this humbly and with the fear my mother instilled in me, should she ever read this. If someone asked my mom what her worst quality is, she'll say that it's being "too nice." In other words, her worst quality is that she's perfect. For the most part, I agree with her; she really is a mild-tempered woman who tries to do no harm (emphasis on tries) and rarely has disagreements with people. The issue is that? If you are a child of my mother and decide to disagree, may you be prepared for the coldest winter ever. My mother perfected ghosting before it was ever a thing. Perhaps that's how she is able to solidify her stance on being the kindest person ever. You won't hear an unkind word from her, you'll just experience silence. And when you follow up on the disappearing act, you're immediately met with kindness. It's a strategy I'm convinced she has down pat. And because for most of my life I didn't understand the power of silence, I spent a lot of time filling the silence with my own opposing points, not realizing that no answer is probably the loudest answer there is.

I would say that these days, she has gotten better at offering a response to disagreement. That's mostly because I've clued her into my knowledge of her "strategy," and although she won't admit to her ghosting, she's ghosting less. I've realized, only now as an adult, that our parents' primary parenting skills are based on how they were parented, and the same goes for their parents, and their parents' parents, and so on and so on up the chain—and down to us. So parenting is just a culmination of the past. I actively try to evaluate if my past parenting makes sense for how I raise my children now.

What I know for sure is that my mom definitely didn't have the time to evaluate whether there were changes to be made in her parenting style while she was raising us. How could she? Like other Black moms raising children in the 1980s and '90s, she was busy raising us and our status in this country. Both required some serious heavy lifting. When we were younger my mom was driving us back and forth every day to magnet schools that were twenty-five miles away, then picking us up for after school activities followed by late night homework time, all while moving up the corporate ladder and, at one point, going back to school.

For some context before I make my point, the Black family steadily rose into the middle- and upper-middle-class income levels during the 1980s and '90s largely because of the work Black moms were putting in. While Black families were laying the groundwork for a new sense of stability, we kids were for the most part being parented from the established groundwork of traditional upbringing. I recently read an article from the American Psychological Association that said that Black families in America have not had the luxury of parenting without the influence and rules under slavery for very long; it's truly been only about 150 years of parenting our children independently.[*] Considering some of our parents can remember segregation and were brought up with grandparents who could recall slavery, the conditions under which Black parents have had to parent and pass down a parenting system have been less than ideal and very limited.

When it came to discipline, I'm happy to say my parents never laid a hand on me. But screaming and raised voices? The norm. I remember one time my mom really had it with me. She screamed so much that my five-year-old self only knew that whatever I did, it must have been really bad. Coincidentally, that week at school we learned about calling 911 on bad people, and that when you called, the police would come and take these bad people away to jail. Well, guess what? My mom's screaming that had me shook? Problem just got solved. I remember thinking

---

[*] Stacey Patton, "Corporal Punishment in Black Communities: Not an Intrinsic Cultural Tradition but Racial Trauma," *CYF News*, April 1, 2017, https://www.apa.org/pi/families/resources/newsletter/2017/04/racial-trauma.

immediately, "Screaming is bad, and if only bad people do bad things, then my mom is a bad person." My five-year-old self was shocked; I mean, I was living with a bad person. Whew! I still feel kind of shocked I conjured up this conclusion. It was bold. But it is what it is. Five-year-olds don't deal in nuanced emotions; they deal in facts told to them by others, and the teacher had just dropped some very useful facts. I needed to call the police on her.

You already know this could not go over well. Because I was five, I didn't know how to use the phone on my own. I needed to have my mom help me call the police. Yes, she needed to dial for me. I came home that day and told my mom that screaming made her a bad person, and I needed to call the police on her so that she could be taken away. I had a plan and she needed to help me. I don't think I ever thought about where she would be taken to or the implications of having her taken away. I just had to be quick with the knowledge I had.

Well, we all know that nothing scares a Black mom. I mean nothing. My mom didn't even blink when I told her. She responded cool, calm, and collected, "Sure." She had no problem with me going ahead and calling 911. I could go right ahead, but first she needed to fill me in on some more information that my teacher might have left out from our lesson today. I was all ears. In my mind, nothing could change my decision. She understood her time screaming at me was coming to an end; this was just a last-minute plan to stall. Or so I thought. Much to my surprise my mom let me know that when 911 comes to get her for "screaming"—because as she recalls, she barely raised her voice but fine she was going with what I said—that they wouldn't be taking her away. No, they would be taking me away! Even if they believed me that she was "screaming," that was the beginning of my problems.

What they would want to do is make sure that I wasn't in harm's way. Calling 911 was a serious thing; they would be taking me away as they evaluated our home and my mom. Again, I was shook. This time more shook than when ScreamingGate occurred. The way my eyes widened, I couldn't blink, let alone breathe. I was not in a bad home. My mom screamed, and that made her a bad person. I was just applying what my teacher taught us.

Now that I am older, I clearly know my mom was talking about me essentially being put in child protective services while they investigated a potential abuse case, and that she was highly exaggerating the level of response that would have happened if 911 came. But back then, all I could think about was being scared of being taken away from my room and, even worse, my toys. Nonetheless, my mom went on with detailing what the next steps would look like when the police came. My little fancy room that I loved so much? None of that was coming with me. And then came the gut punch of all gut punches: I'd have to share a room with someone.

Oh hell no, this was not what I had in mind at all. Everyone knew that I hated sharing, so I didn't know if she was throwing that in just to scare me, but it didn't matter. I wasn't going to risk it. I knew enough; the call wouldn't be happening. I quickly apologized for even mentioning calling 911 and went to my room to cry. My mom essentially gave me what I call Classic Old-School Black Mom: "Test me and I will test you." As she liked to say, "I am not one of your little friends." And at five years old, I learned to never threaten to call the police on my mom again.

I can look back on that situation now and see the humor. I don't feel it was as terrible as I felt it was at five, but I still have an uneasy feeling about screaming in general. Screaming, to me, seems so normal in parenting in general and admittedly was very normal in my childhood. I'm not going to lie, I still scream. When I'm frustrated, irritated, or angry, I scream. I probably scream for more reasons than that, if I'm being truthful. I feel bad every time I scream, and especially if I scream at my kids. I imagine my mom felt bad too, but at the same time, she probably felt it was necessary. Like it was necessary to be heard, especially over my crying or to show power over whatever behavior she was trying to correct. That's what comes to mind for me at least when I think about why I scream.

In an odd way, it's meant to be correct. To correct a "bad" behavior with another "bad" behavior, the irony. Also, because my parents never beat me, I imagine screaming seemed like a good alternative. In comparison to what my mom experienced growing up, she probably wished someone just screamed at her instead of all the beatings she experienced. I used to get on my mom about her screaming because I felt like she was completely unaware that she was doing it, and, similar to ghosting, she rarely admits to doing it. But I've realized I scream too much in the same way. So I've stopped confronting her about it. It's a not-so-great learned behavior that admittedly I'm not always doing the best at controlling.

Screaming to correct someone's, and in this case a child's, negative behavior, in my opinion, is like trying to solve one negative action with another. Will it scare them, and maybe even you? Hell, yes. Does it have the permanent effect you're looking for? Likely not. How often did I used to find myself doing the same thing I was just screamed at for? We all can relate, it's just a matter of time before the effect of the screaming starts to wear off or becomes emotionally traumatizing. The underlining problem it was trying to solve? Likely still there.

Recently, I was screaming at my toddler about something in what I'd call not my best mommy moment. I was stressed, tired, and unfortunately it happened. Out of nowhere my son boldly and frantically interrupted me with "Mommy! Mommy!" I paused and yelled, "What!" He then gathered his three-year-old composure and said slowly and clearly to ensure he had my attention, "Friends don't scream at friends, Mommy."

That stopped me in my tracks. He was right; friends don't scream at friends. But what was also important and, honestly, jarring for me is that he said "friends." My son thinks I'm his friend. I was immediately overjoyed and heartbroken. Overjoyed because despite my screaming, which I am working on, and whatever other parenting guilt I may have had about not being the best mom, he thought I was worthy enough to be his friend. And here I was screaming at my friend.

Knowing I grew up in the "I'm not your little friend" generation, this was significant. I can't even recall the countless times I heard that statement. Although I understood it, I never enjoyed it. I knew I didn't want to continue it with my kids, and so far it hasn't. I've also, until this point, never explicitly told my son he was my friend, so the fact that he gathered that sentiment about our relationship on his own meant a lot to me. Somehow my intention of creating a trusting environment that he feels comfortable being all parts of himself, even with my screaming mishaps, was coming through. It warmed my heart that my little baby felt comfortable enough to call me a friend and wanted better friend behavior from me, his friend, as he should. Screaming was doing nothing to improve our relationship now or help create the one that I wanted to have with my son in the future.

I learn so much from the little humans who call me Mommy. This has allowed me to be comfortable with my own reparenting, and we should all be comfortable learning from our children, regardless of their age. Reparenting doesn't have to wait a generation, for when we feel like our children are older or more credible. Their feelings, their experiences, are credible and teachable moments for us and for them at any and all points in their lives. As a Black mom, I've been intentional on doubling down on this way of thinking for myself. I also think of the effects this will have on my children. I think about my own life as a Black woman and how often my lived experiences were automatically undervalued. Your feelings being validated as credible should start at home.

Let's go deeper into the thinking on this. How many times out in the world have our likes and dislikes have been disregarded? Why should our children also have to come home to that? We don't want to be early contributors to those feelings of invalidation. Our homes should be safe havens our kids can count on. Personally, I want to raise children who know that what they feel and have experienced is being heard. They will be better stewards of themselves when the world says otherwise. So when we get feedback from our kids—which we all know can happen often in toddler land of big exploding feelings—we should do our best and not be afraid to adjust how we respond in recognition of what they are telling us they feel. It's not about power. It's not about control. It's about seeing our kids as human and important as they are, and as they grow.

Reparenting ourselves is also about respecting boundaries. My youngest son mastered "No!" and "Go away!" very early on. And while it looks and sounds as hilarious as you could imagine having a little human with an Afro bigger than his head who can barely walk scream these things at you, it for sure stops you in your tracks. But "no" and "go away" are real and valid feelings that people can have and do have. Our goal should be to help them understand when those feelings arise and find valid responses to them. Suppressing "no" in my children does not help them protect their boundaries in the future.

My own internal wiring has begun to calm down when I get these types of responses from my son. I am less bothered and spend more time observing what is going on when my child is making these proclamations. Of course, I'm not going away and leaving a one-year-old unattended because he demands it. But I am going to make sure he's safe and, when there's the option to, giving him the space to play or just meander around independently. You know what is surprising for me? Even at one, he is fully aware of when he wants his own space. When I see his little face light up, I know that this self-awareness is not something I want to scream out of him.

You know how many times I have wanted to do just like my youngest son and tell people "No" or "Go away"? Plenty. Do I actually do that? More times than not, I don't. There are so many times even now as an adult that I can't quite muster up the courage to say what I want. To ask for my space, to say, "Actually, no I don't like that," or just to say no without an explanation.

Boundaries, at times, have been super difficult and uncomfortable for me to enforce. But watching my youngest push away foods he doesn't want or swat away unwanted attention or affection reminds me that we are born with boundaries. Over time, with every forced interaction or invalidated feeling, those boundaries are eroded. And then as adults, we are forced to find them again. I'm not trying to intentionally erode anyone's boundaries.

I'm not saying that my children are living a free-for-all here either. Rules for their safety must exist, and they should be followed. As the person who is responsible for these kids, I must enforce those rules. At times they don't like that, but the goal is to make sure they grow with safe boundaries and learn to set their own parameters when they are adults. Watching my youngest son's unbiased objections to what he doesn't want and clear declarations of what he does has sparked a little more courage in me these days. Of course, I aim to make my delivery calmer and more respectful—and I've successfully been able to get my no's heard more often.

The youngest members of our family's ability to shift generational behaviors has been monumental and noticeable. Most significant, it has been in the expression of affection. In some Black families, kids heard they were loved from someone every day. In others, like mine, I knew I was loved but the act of saying "I love you" was scarce and reserved for special occasions. It just isn't a natural thing to just say. I figured my parents never said it because people in their families didn't say it a lot. "I love you" has been passed down as an implicitly understood emotion, not one expressed verbally. Growing up, I think I desired the verbal "I love you" more than I admittedly knew. Being in relationships where saying it was a noteworthy step made me realize that desire even more.

And even though growing up I never felt unloved, I knew I wanted my children to hear the words affirming it every day and not have to assume that was what I was feeling. Reparenting is exactly that, recognizing that some behaviors from the past are not ones we want to carry into the future. It's affirming and continuing all the things that made us feel like uplifted Black girls and now Black women and reevaluating the thing that don't. There is space in every generation to evaluate what no longer works for them and for that to be OK. I wholly expect my sons to find a way of parenting that works for them, should they choose to have a family. What I know is that I am a mom to sons. I really want my sons to experience all of what it is to have Black boy joy, day in and day out. And for me, that starts with audibly saying "I love you" and creating an environment in which it isn't awkward for them to do so too.

And you know who's been saying "I love you" these days? My parents. I like to believe it started because of how my husband and I normalized saying it to our sons, which in turn made it natural for my sons to say it to their grandma and grandpa, even if it's being used as a ploy for "more treats," as my toddler says. Or maybe it's because becoming grandparents has opened up a feeling of new unconditional love again in my parents? Either way I'll take it.

Children can make so many long-standing

behaviors and ways of doing things feel like they need correction. They offer an opportunity to do things differently, to revisit how you felt experiencing certain things and adjusting for a different outcome for the next generation. What's interesting is that this evaluation doesn't only have to come from children. It can come from ourselves. These days, I'm happy I give myself the opportunity to have a do-over in how I treat myself, or how I desire others to treat me. My inner child is always reparenting itself. Some behaviors that were passed down or natural to me, be it from childhood or adulthood, don't quite sit right with me. I have no problem putting them up for evaluation. I have no problem being and doing different than I did before.

———————

It's easy to grasp that sometimes our parents need reparenting and that we, as Black women, should think about ways we can break away from generational parenting norms that may not have worked for us. But what if one of our reparenting tools also looks like not answering every call? If in our other relationships we can choose which interactions are worth our efforts, why can't the same be true in the relationship with our parents?

I know the first thought is going to be, "Black people don't do things like that! We don't intentionally ignore our parents or choose not to interact with them. You know how bad that's going to look for the family?" And for a lot of us, those statements are true. But just like other relationships that may not serve us, not all the interactions we have with our parents serve us either. There is no blanket rule that says they should. We have the right to decide when we want to pull away by not answering every call so that we can preserve ourselves, the relationship, or both. We can end the generational norm of being participants to every interaction.

This is in no way intended to be disrespectful to our parents or to end the relationship we have with them. As adults who make decisions in every other part of our lives about what serves us and what doesn't, we should trust ourselves enough to know that, even with our parents, we can make and institute boundaries that are based on what we know about them, us, and the relationship. Our past experiences can guide us on what the outcome may be and if it is more desirable to not end up there.

Sometimes my mom will see me parenting in ways that are different from hers and make comments of disapproval or comparison to her parenting. More times than not these days, I do not respond. Why? Because it won't positively affect anything. Do I intend to change the way I have chosen to parent? No. Will it more than likely be met with more conflict? Yes. Me answering that call in that situation just invites more resistance and possibly conflict. Also, as I plan to continue on and parent in the way that works for me and my child, both myself and my child maintain the relationship we have. Imagine introducing a new way to parent or discipline to my child solely based on a comment that was made. That would be so disruptive to them emotionally and behaviorally. Responding to every interaction, comment, or suggestion from our parents is the same; it can be disruptive to us emotionally and, at times, alter the way we behave—"Hello, I'm feeling some type of way so now I'm not picking up the phone next time you call."

The fear we may have about pulling away or not interacting with our parents and particularly our mothers, as Black women, is a reaction to an unspoken rule of generational parenting. It's so rigid that at times we can be absolutely destroyed emotionally by our parents and still return to the fire, so to speak. Taking the time to step back is not about severing your mother/daughter or parent/daughter relationship. I'm not saying to call it quits if overall it is a beneficial and healthy relationship. I'm saying consider how you can preserve what's great about those relationships (and yourself) when you do have to take time to pull away.

If you're like me, you are not going to see eye to eye on everything with your parents or parental figures, but guess what? That's OK. Sometimes it is hard for our parents, or us for that matter, to switch out of disciplinary parenting mode and see us as adults. Seeing your child, no matter their age, make decisions that don't align with yours triggers the need to direct and discipline. It is natural for them to go into disciplinary mode, especially since they've been doing it for so long. What's often unnatural to them is understanding that you are making choices and decisions that work for you; that is a learned behavior that's hard to break.

I'm still learning to be open to that with my young children. There are things for them even as toddlers that work better for them than what even I suggest. For example, the other day I was insisting my four-year-old wear shorts that were made out of khaki material. I felt he looked more put together, and since they were shorts they were still casual. After lots of crying—and I mean lots—he finally said, "Mommy, I want to wear the soft shorts because I want to jump and run fast when I play."

I immediately knew exactly what he meant when he said that. The khaki, although shorts, were a more restrictive material and at four years old, his priority is playing and running and jumping, not looking like you're ready for a business interview. I relented and let him wear his athletic jersey material shorts as soon as it clicked for me. He knew better than me what he needed and what worked for him in that moment.

You know how some comments come off as a smart comment or ready for conflict? I get these all the time from my mom, or at least it feels like that's what they are. Lately, I've stopped trying to analyze if they are that or not and focus on trying to keep what's good about our relationship intact, not being in a rush to respond since it would then put us both in defensive mode. Not responding or taking the time to respond most of the time results in me just continuing on without feeling the need to address what is said and, trust me, sometimes the comments I get from my mom feel like the type you could only get from a Black mom. I know you know what I mean. The ones that feel like they know exactly what to say to cut at the right moment. But if I don't feel like responding will be beneficial to our relationship, I just don't respond.

You know what I also don't do? Wait for an apology or an acknowledgment of the action. Now, don't get me wrong, sometimes I throw all of that out the door and the call is short and to the point.

A while ago I heard the phrase "forgiveness is for you" in regards to how you heal yourself and the negative feelings you may have. I feel the same way about apologies from our parents. A big part of reparenting ourselves is having the knowledge that a lot of the actions that disappoint us about our parents would be different if they had better tools at their disposal. When is the last time you've heard your parents apologize? If your parents are like mine, then you know apologizing is like kryptonite to them. Knowing that an apology may never come doesn't mean you have to accept the behaviors or things said that make you feel some kind of way. I don't. It also doesn't mean you need to continue to be around those behaviors.

Remember, don't feel tempted to answer that call.

What it does mean is that you have a good understanding of what works and doesn't work for you without an apology, and if you need to move on from a situation or person, parents included, you can do that. It goes back to my therapist repeating "So what?" to me when I try to mentally stick around for things that are said about me or to me by other people. So what? Make the decisions that best serve you. Sometimes the biggest peace we can give ourselves in the reparenting journey is a quick mental "So what?" or refocusing as we recenter ourselves and maintain what we know about ourselves and the person we are.

Reparenting ourselves and any efforts to reparent our parents can feel like extreme work. In all of it, we deserve grace and the option to opt out when we want. Yes, Black girl, you can opt out! Remember when my mother-in-law decided she would call us back when it was best for her to do so? Our parents have been opting out and choosing what's right for them. You can do the same; the process in no way should feel restrictive.

I think about how often we don't allow ourselves do-overs, resets, second chances, especially as Black women. For me it was rooted in perfection, fear of change, or even worse, fear of rejection, or a search for power. How did I find comfort in my consistent tries at reparenting? Well, part of the process is accepting that there are changes that I want to make that I will always have some discomfort around. Like not always having to be the be-all, end-all authority on everything and being unquestionable. As Black women, do we need this extra responsibility? I know for me this is what I saw growing up so that is what I did. But now I'm getting used to being vulnerable in front of my children and using phrases like "That's a good question" versus "Because I said so." That all-knowing power, that ain't me. I'm not going to force an answer just to have one.

There are things I absolutely know and things my children must absolutely do while I'm raising them that pertain to their overall health and safety. That is my responsibility. Everything else, there's a lot of grey area there. Spending less time asserting ourselves and leaning into that level of vulnerability with our children is a good thing. It allows them to practice grace and compassion when their mommy doesn't know everything, and to feel comfortable seeking the same. Because of that, their no's are also intertwined with "I don't knows."

Navigating reparenting has as much to do with our parents as it does with ourselves. There are some things I know I would love for my parents to do differently or wished they would have done differently, but I don't have that control over them, or anyone for that matter. I have control over myself and so do you. There are boundaries that I keep that are an example to my children. There are also behaviors that I model that lead to better outcomes. The boundaries and outcomes I actively keep and seek day in and day out demonstrate not only the way I parent but also what I desire in regard to being parented and treated overall. Sometimes it works and sometimes it doesn't. And gracefully, I take the wins with the losses. What there has been is an overall improvement in my relationship with my parents and the confidence I feel in my own ability to parent.

Truth #10

Our Relationship with Money Is Petty

Look, I love a new outfit, a hot off the flat iron silk press and, of course, fresh braids. And fresh vacation braids? Even better. Nothing can stop me when I feel confident in how I look. Add to the occasion a just-washed car, new mani-pedi, and glistening moisturized skin, and I'm pretty much unstoppable.

Black women should never apologize for looking good. Never. And about the time it takes to do so? Also be unapologetic. I've come to realize that if you want the best version of me, I need to feel my best. So even though these days, when I don't have as much time to myself to get everything done from my head to my toes, from my car to my house, I plan for these things here and there. Time and money spent on yourself is always a good investment.

It's like that "nothing can stop me now" feeling you get when you spend a Saturday at the mall and it is just going your way. Everything you try on is looking right, and you know all the places you are going to wear your new outfits. Store after store, you're stacking designer bags, like who's that girl? You're feeling like you've transported yourself back to the early '90s and you're Dionne in *Clueless*. Yes, girl, those shopping trips can give me life too. It's as if the shopping gods knew I was coming. And the labels, don't get me started. I love Target, but I also love a good designer label. My style is more the incognito label type. If you know the signature cut or style, then you know who it is. I'm not the repetitive monogram type but to each his own. I appreciate all of it. I remember when Louboutins were gaining popularity and it was like every Black girl had a pair. You couldn't enter a room of Black women without half their heels being red bottoms and their bags being Louis V. It was like someone sent a signal out to all of us to make sure we had the shoes and bags, basically the new Black girl uniform for years.

Of course, whether all of this is your cup or tea or not is your prerogative. But the judgmental comments on other people's spending choices? Nauseating—and even more nauseating when it's Black women being commented on. As if we need more judgment. No, sir, we do not. What makes me even more bothered than judgmental comments on Black women spending? When those comments come from other Black women. Is it out of concern, sis? If not, let that person live. If it is, great. We really do need more transparent conversations about money between us.

I love that we can spend and treat ourselves. For me that's part of removing the assumptions about where society thinks we should be economically. But what I don't love? For a long while I had no sounding board, no group of girlfriends that I could have transparent conversations with about money. Not conversations about where to go all out on retail therapy and "treat yo' self" indulgences; I'm talking about money talks that change how Black girls now, and in the future, continue to improve our financial status and money smarts.

Talking about money has always been taboo in some circles. And among Black folks, that has historically been the case. Especially in front of older generations, it feels like a betrayal of an unspoken code. I think it's time to have those money conversations without the gasps or the looks that could kill that come with it. Black women, the most influential group of consumers on the planet, are definitely the ones who need to be having them. We can't be moving the needle in so many areas of our lives and not be moving the needle to normalize these conversations.

Let me tell you how nonexistent money conversations are in some Black families using mine as an example. I'll take one for the team and assume my ancestors are somewhere gasping at the audacity of me doing so. In my family, we don't have transparent money conversations for even the most basic things. To this day we still have the occasional trip up, as I call it, when the larger family group is planning on hosting a holiday, birthday, or celebration. Very often we follow the understood rule: the person who invites everyone is the one who bears all the costs. But every so often we run into the "we all are planning this event" scenario, so the clear who's-in-charge and who's-paying-for-what gets lost in the who's-baking-the-mac-and-cheese or the who's-bringing-the-rice-and-peas. And if oxtails are being made? Get ready for a full financial bailout followed by reconstruction of burnt bridges being needed, if no one offers to share the cost of that dish right away.

Year after year, and "we are all hosting" this event after "we are all hosting" this event, the same thing occurs. The event is planned, everyone's hosting, people decide what they are bringing or contributing, the event ends, and the resentful conversations begin. I've heard everything from "I didn't expect for the oxtail to have so much bone; I shouldn't have given So- 'n'-So that much money toward it" to the "they don't appreciate [this pricey food item], so next time I'm not going to spend so much money and make it." No one completely falls out of the family for it, but it can create awkward moments until they forget about it for the next family gathering around the corner, only to do it all over again.

Perhaps that's just family dynamics in general but I can't help thinking how much less awkward it would be and how much more enjoyable a time we would have if, upfront, people stated the limits of their contributions to these events or the expectations they had for their contributions. Things like, "How many people will all of this oxtail serve before I give you this money?" or "Do you and your kids eat [this pricey food item]? Let me know so I don't make a lot of it." It sounds so basic but my family would rather skirt around these essential questions because talking about money is taboo. I can imagine the same is true in so many other Black families.

So let's talk about money. As you know, I'm your blunt friend. For me talking about money just has to be brought up, without hesitance or pause. It's the ripping the Band-Aid off type of way to introduce the conversation to your group of friends or your family, wherever the conversation needs to be had. Will people be uncomfortable? Yes. Will some relationships be altered? Potentially. But what's more injurious? Constantly feeling some type of way, or saying something and it not immediately going the way you think it should? There are different ways to bring up these conversations. Some of them can happen organically and others may happen as a result of you actively setting boundaries around your financial decisions or, even more encouraging, a conversation can turn into a group effort. There are so many ways to approach us having a better relationship with money and talking about it. Here are a few that may be helpful.

The "Right in the Middle of the Mess" Approach

Sometimes we're in the middle of a money mess. Maybe we're out at a restaurant, splitting a check with a group of friends. You know how it goes, with that one person who orders one of everything plus multiple drinks but is the first to speak up about splitting the check evenly. Or maybe we're in the middle of planning a family trip and no one is going anywhere because no one wants to take the risk of putting their card up to pay for things (since we all know a certain somebody never pays people back). These are the moments we are in the middle of the mess. And they're the perfect time, if you are prepared, to create a change of habit for that moment and for the future.

How does that look in practice? In our first scenario, you're out with girlfriends and splitting the check equally doesn't feel equal, especially because some people indulged more than others. Interject. Say something like: "Hey ladies, I think I may have overindulged a bit." Even if you didn't, you're just breaking the ice here. "Let me see how much I owe, and then I'll take care of that separately." You've started, by being the example, splitting the bill based on what everyone actually ordered.

In our second scenario, of family trip planning, interject the same way. Try, "Hey, it looks like the total amount is x dollars. I'll transfer my portion to whoever plans on putting it on their card. When they get everyone's money, they can reserve the house for us." You're paying for your obligation up front, and suggesting a healthy action everyone else should take before the trip is booked that doesn't leave the financial burden on one person.

Let's also not be naive here and think that it is always going to be easy to break up the money scramble right in the middle of things. You know that you can make the best effort to get people to pay up front or pay for what they are responsible for and it still ain't going to work. The truth is, you know who those people are. If its an issue you don't want to deal with, you're just going to have to stop interacting with them in that way if it is consequential to you. What do I mean? If you know someone likes to spend more than they hold themselves accountable for when they go out with the group, and there are no signs of them changing even with an intervention that encourages everyone to pay their portion, then that is who that person is and you're not going to change that. So before you go out with that person, your budget should take that into account, or you should not go out to places with them in which your budget can't accommodate for their underpayment.

There are friends I have that I will not invite to certain places. We are no less friends because of that but I am not going to put our friendship on the line by inviting them to places I know will create a conflict in our relationship—places that I know they will leave me hanging with a bill I don't want to have to fully cover. The same goes with trips and splitting costs. As this Black girl IRL has gotten more educated about my personal finances and what I can afford, gone are the days of going on every and any girl's trip. Yes, I said it. Girls' trips that have major costs that will be split, like accommodations or transportation that is not paid in advance, or that I know will have a straggler or two on the payments, I'm not going on. Last thing I want to be is the sponsor on a girls' trip. The same rule applies for me on family trips. I know the family members whose costs I will cover (read: the people that live in my house, and whoever I may be treating) and that's it.

We will not be on a fully sponsored family reunion on my dime.

The "It's Not Within My Budget" Approach

Ever have a friend or group of friends that every time you're around them, you find yourself having to keep up like they're the Joneses? Every invitation to participate in the friendship with them seems like an opportunity to spend money, or even more so, spend more money than you'd like to. It may not even be a consistent thing, but it's enough that you don't feel too great about the financial aftermath of participating in the things they like to do. I say this is the best scenario to be blunt in. "No, it's not within my budget," and, "I'd rather not attend things that are going to cost me x," are both perfect answers. It also makes it clear to the person or people you're with that you are not willing to go outside your financial boundaries.

And for that one girlfriend who likes to bring up all the other things you've spent money on recently, or in the past, so why can't you make the sacrifice just this one time? "I've made my decision but thank you again for inviting me," will have to be a good enough answer for her. There's always that someone, whether it be in your friend circle or family, who thinks they know your budget better than you do. There's no need to fight them on the knowledge they think they have. It's a call you don't have to answer. But what you can do is reiterate that your decision has been made and you're sticking with it, regardless of their pushback or feelings of insider knowledge on your financial situation.

I've set my boundary in the past and, surprisingly, oftentimes the same friend who was pressuring me to spend above my budget or bringing up all the things I do budget for will respond in the likes of "Me too, girl, I get it." It's like they were only willing to go past their own financial boundaries if someone else was willing to participate in it with them.

The "not within my budget" approach works the other way too. You can initiate the budget conversation. I love it when someone gives me an idea of how much something is going to cost if it's a new experience or place we've not gone to together. A simple "It's going to cost x to do this," or, "If we go here, it's generally around x dollars. Is that within your budget?" are ways to allow others to openly see if something fits within their boundaries of spending. I invite people out like this often. If it's with a group, even better. Gone are the headaches of the surprise bill that no one wants to split because who knew So-'n'-So was going to drink half the tab. Setting the expectation for the group ahead of time about what costs are associated with something or encouraging them to bring cash to facilitate splitting the bill tells everyone up front what it's going to be.

I don't know about you but it is so much more

relaxing to enjoy time with friends and loved ones when you know that there's not going to be tension about money. Everyone has an expectation going into how much things will cost.

The "Let's Do This Together" Approach

Funny thing is, more times than not, our friends and family are open to doing things toward a goal together. Financial planning and budgeting are one of the things that can be fun, if it's a group effort. Teaming up with friends or family to do things such as eating out fewer times per month, limiting frivolous spending for some time period, or even reading a personal finance book as part of a book club are good ways to do something beneficial for the betterment of everyone's future. I've never been invited to a budget challenge and turned it down, because the truth is there's always an opportunity to improve my spending.

Ever think about even making the most daunting tasks when it comes to budgeting a fun experience? How about invite some girlfriends over for some wine with a dedicated financial betterment task on the docket, like cleaning up all those subscriptions and memberships that you have. Subscriptions and memberships tend to auto-renew, and it's easy to forget about them when we no longer use them (hello gym membership I haven't used in three years). The same goes for credit cards; we tend to gravitate toward using one or two cards while the others may

sit around unused or lightly used and we are still paying an annual membership fee for them. Make it an
encouraging environment to get through the not so
fun task of getting your financial house in order peri-
odically by inviting your girlfriends to do the same.

———————

I had my rude awakening with bad money management or the lack of money management shortly after
I graduated from undergrad. I never talked about
money, it wasn't talked about around me, and the
effects of how badly I mismanaged my money lasted
me for years. My first job out of school was working
in finance for a great company making $55K a year.
They even gave me a $10K relocation budget on top
of that the first year so that I could move and get settled into the city where they were located. At barely
twenty-one years old, and having only worked hourly
jobs before that, I felt I was doing pretty well with
that salary. Thinking about it now, even by today's
standards, for someone coming straight out of undergrad with no experience, that was a more than fair
salary. They'd really bet on my success, and the pay
they offered me proved it.

A month before I started working, I drove to my
new city with my mom and found what was to be
my first apartment. It was perfect, a one-bedroom/
one-bathroom for $975 a month. I quickly did the
math and $55,000 divided by twelve was about
$4,500 a month. I didn't account for taxes, 401(k),

or anything. I thought, *How much could they really take out for taxes?* I felt I had more than enough money. I signed the lease for my apartment that same day. They did a quick check of my credit, and I used my sign-on bonus to pay for the deposit and security payment.

Now it was time for me to get a car. I couldn't believe how wealthy I was at twenty-one. I didn't know of Mark Zuckerberg and I had no real wealthy twenty-one-year-olds to compare wealth with, so to me, I was wealthy and I was going to find the perfect car to match my new status. A week later, I purchased what would be my first car that I would pay for on my own, a brand new Acura. For $502.26 a month, it was mine. With my quick math—that, again, didn't account for taxes or withholdings—after I paid for my apartment and new car, I still had money to burn. I was rich.

About a month into the new job, I was doing well on my team, had a good circle of friends, and was really liking the post-college life. It was similar to undergrad; during the day I was working, but at night and on weekends, and with no responsibilities other than myself, I was out enjoying time with my friends. Happy hours, late night club outings, week-end brunches, I was in all of it. And what goes best with a life of leisure, as I called that period of my time? A fly wardrobe and trips to match.

At first, I paid for all of my expenditures right out of my bank account. I never had a credit card before and didn't see the need to get one. But a few months into my new job and lifestyle, the credit card companies figured out where I lived. Offer after offer noted my excellent credit, because I paid my car on time. I'd never gotten mail like this before. I didn't fully understand it, but I thought I knew the basics; you get a credit card, you buy stuff, you pay the bill for the credit card. Easy. I picked the card offer I liked best, based on nothing other than one with the highest credit limit, and off to spending I went.

When I say you couldn't tell me nothing, I really mean it. I was ballin' hard and spending heavy. Let me note that this was all before the Instagram era, but when I go back and see those many photos I have of my friends and me "living the life" and "out and about," I realize the price tag of those days was in the thousands. Think about that. This is me and my little digital Casio camera, also purchased with my credit card, and what must have been tons of HD cards uploaded to my computer. Spending was the new lifestyle. It felt like power and a release. I could assert my independence as an adult, because people trusted adults with credit cards, and I now had one. Life after undergrad was better than I could imagine.

I remember the day that euphoria came to an abrupt halt. My mom called me frantic on a Saturday. She had just received a credit card bill to her house with my name on it, and it had a $17,000 balance. Someone had stolen my personal information and taken out a card in my name and ran up all these charges! I needed to call the number from the credit card statement immediately. She couldn't believe this was happening to me. She had no idea, and neither did I to be honest, that the "thief" was me. I mean, I obviously knew that I was the one using the card, but I had no idea I'd taken my newfound "wealth" to this extent. The cost of my new freedom as an adult was astronomical.

I had her read out what some of the transactions were just so I could confirm what I already knew. Macy's, Expedia, restaurant, restaurant, Macy's again, Bloomingdale's; they all sounded familiar. I had to tell her it was me. And if I thought talking about anything money-related felt shameful before, admitting to my spending spree and subsequent debt was worse than any conversation about money I'd ever experienced before. It was met with a lot of questions, such as "What could you be buying?" "Where are these things you are buying?" and most important, "Who will be paying for this bill?" I had few answers. I felt like I'd messed up everything in such a short period of time.

I would like to say that I got a hold of my spending and immediately paid the bill off but that definitely wasn't the case. A lot of that money I had "calculated" I would be taking home was not there obviously. All those taxes that had to be withheld already brought down my monthly paycheck by a third. And oh yeah, having an apartment on my own was more expensive than I'd planned for. Water bill, electric bill, cable bill, parking pass—all of that added up. My $975 rent? Double that for all the associated expenses. And don't even get me started on my fancy new Acura,

$502.26; that number haunted me until I finally paid the car off—that's why I still know it by heart. I didn't buy another car for ten years because I was so scarred by those payments.

It took me five years to pay off that card. Yes, five years. I spent all five years paying the minimum balance because I really could not afford to pay the card and maintain all the other expenses I had. The balance never moved an inch. I didn't pay it off until year five, and that was with my sign on bonus from my first job after grad school.

I think about how if I knew better, I would have done better. During those five years, despite how many other things were going on, that debt was always lingering in the background. To say it was stressful is an understatement. All through graduate school as a full-time student, I had that debt. I had to find a way to continue making minimum payments while I had no income. For me that meant having to liquidate the 401(k) I had amassed from my previous job. I was in survival mode in one part of my life while trying to move forward in other parts.

I have no idea how the other people in my friend circle were affording the lifestyle we were all living. Maybe some were making more than I was, or others had better saving and investing knowledge than I did. Or maybe some were just like me, overusing their credit cards. But what I do know was that there was never a budget for anything. We never checked in with each other about if we were all cool spending and splurging on our next adventure, be it happy hour or vacation. Whatever the cost, we were all always down for it.

The depth of the money conversations we should be having goes beyond the price of nights out, vacations, and rent. I remember the salary of my first job not because it was the most I've ever made but because it was the first time someone wanted to pay me for what they thought my ability was and what I could bring to the table. Looking back, I would have benefitted from having a true understanding of salary negotiation and how much I should have been paid.

Cultivating a trusted circle of other women working in the same or similar industry as you that you can confide in is a great step toward getting that transparency around salaries and salary negotiations. And if these women are at varying points in their career, even better. I know that if I'm able to share with other Black women my experience with a particular company or role, I'm happy to. The idea that they would be taking from what is available to me if I do so is limiting. The reality is that salary and financial transparency is alive in many other communities outside of the Black community, and we need to get on the page that this transparency is needed for us as well. There's no better way to increase our Black wealth than to have a diverse perspective of what your experience commands, and that involves getting perspective from within our community and outside of it as well.

My perspective is if we can't talk about money, then how can we get more of it? It's hard to get more of something that you don't discuss with other people since, in general, money is offered in exchanges of value. I want to hear and talk about all of these exchanges of value. I want to know if I can afford it or not. I want to know how to grow my value and when I need to save it. So how do we as Black women promote these dialogues more among ourselves? We just have to start having them and being comfortable that they may be uncomfortable.

One of the biggest helps for opening up transparent conversations in my friendships has been utilizing one of the approaches I mentioned earlier and checking in to ask, "Does this work for everyone's budget?" If anything, what I learned from my trips and travels on a credit card life was that I went along with every budget because there was no budget. No one asked. It sounds simple, but we were all just going along unchecked. Checking the budget and if it aligns for everyone, whether we are meeting up for dinner or taking a girls' trip, makes the whole experience that much better. No one is resentful that they are spending money they don't have or going home to a bill that is going to put a strain on their life. That check-in means that if it doesn't work for everyone, we can find a better solution. Or, if the person wants to, they can decline and catch up with us the next time. What's great is there's no shade or shame. I'm not hesitant to decline if I need to. I'd rather do that then end up with years of debt because I was trying to keep up with everyone else.

Money conversations also don't have to be an

intense, planned-out event or a total betrayal of cultural norms. They can be presented as questions ("Does this amount work for you?" or "What is the investment needed to hire you?"), as a place to share ("I paid x for this" or "It can cost between this and this"), or can provide a new perspective ("Typically in this role a person with x experience should be compensated above x amount"). Any way the conversations are had or presented, so much is gained.

I would have loved having all these questions, phrases, and points of view available to me when I was figuring it out, but now that we have started them, sis, let's not be hesitant to keep them going. They will only make all of us better.

Truth #11

It's Gon' Be All Right

For what seems like forever, Black women have had to navigate our way around negativity. In the hierarchy of passing the buck along, Black women are the last to catch it, and there's no one to pass it to. We have had to show one face to the world, smiling on the outside while experiencing everything else inside. But still, as Black women we seem to be able to take an enemy, a hater, or a just awful experience and create a positive shift that moves us forward. Time and time again, that has been us and that's how I know the truth is, we ultimately are going to be all right. Ancestrally most of us have heard a version of this truth at some time or another, but do we really believe it?

I know we should because personally, situations in my life have unfolded from negative into what was truly meant to be—sometimes instantly and sometimes over a prolonged period of time. And it may not have always been what I was initially looking for but it has always been what was right. Sometimes it's growth, other times it's clarity, all the time it was what

I needed. Don't get me wrong, in those moments the light at the end of the tunnel feels unreal. Whether it be career setbacks, relationship fumbles, or "ish" that just makes life feel like a struggle, it feels like the universe has to throw a "Yes, Black girl, you are great, you are wonderful, you are worthy, but wait we aren't ready for that so let us throw you yet another test to see if you can still thrive." That's when we must remain steadfast in the belief of ourselves that yes, we are going to be all right. The friction, the opposition, and of course the haters are going to come and yes we will still thrive. If anything, that friction, that thing blowing against us, like the pressure of the wind needed for a plane to lift off, will raise us up and take us in the direction we need to go.

I don't say this so we can just live life in a state of suspended bliss, hoping for things to just line up or manifest. Behind every manifestation is the work that needs to keep being done. The results, the part that ends with us being all right, comes while you're doing. Some of our biggest letdowns often turn into our biggest opportunities. That's how I know this truth, spoken into our ancestral being, is one we as Black women should lean into.

I remember what I consider my first and biggest failure. It was when I explored entrepreneurship with friends. The way that business failed—what we'd put together was epic, but even worse was how those relationships failed. It had me questioning everything at the time. Ultimately, after much time, everything and everyone ended up all right and I'd venture to say better than all right. Not because the business was no longer a failure or because the relationships were repaired but because of the lessons that came out of that failure. I learned how important clarity is no matter what you assume or what you think you know just because you know someone. I also learned that not everyone, despite how close you are, is motivated in the same way you are. Yes, even among Black girls, we have different motivations. That clarity may have brought me out of that part of my life sooner if I'd known it earlier, but that was the time for me to learn that lesson. Sometimes to get to the all right part of life, lessons will have to be learned, no matter how difficult or painful they may be.

Ever feel like some lessons never end? It's just a season, not a lifetime. Knowing that there are seasons of lessons and seasons when everything is all right is what we as Black women should remain clear on. This too shall pass, sis. It will. This clarity keeps our goals in sight and locked in. I wish I had this clarity when I was younger. I may have not continued on in as many cringe-worthy relationships, waiting for them to improve, or spent as long not speaking up in my career about what I really wanted. I felt like staying in bad relationships was me openly denying that things were bad and proclaiming that they were going to work. Of course, we all know that's not how it goes. Nonetheless, I'm thankful those seasons have come to an end.

Similarly, I remember a time when I just knew I wanted to leave my job because of how awful I felt my then manager was. I interviewed in every city except where I ultimately ended up living, and still live now, because I didn't want to go back to my hometown. I was determined to find a new and better job anywhere but there. And as the universe would have it, I remained in that season of searching for a new job for two years. It felt miserable. It wasn't until I reluctantly accepted an interview in my hometown that I actually found the job and the boss I was looking for and that I needed. Needless to say, it was the beginning of me moving back closer to my immediate family, meeting my husband, and having my children. Things turned out more than all right. I spent those two years resisting what ultimately turned out to be what was best for me. How many things do we resist and are reluctant to try because we don't want to "give in"? Are we prolonging some seasons because we're not being flexible and open? Maybe that thing we're resisting is being presented to us because it is what we need to be all right. It may be just what we need to deliver us from one tough season and into the next phase of our lives.

As Black women we definitely know how to weather these storms. How often do we stop weathering the storm and stand in it though? Standing in the storm can be the release we need. Standing still is so necessary at times to get to the other side. And the storm—for some of us, that is our everyday lives. Juggling career, friendships, family, and all the other obligations. We are everything for so many people. We are literally the definition of hustle and grind culture, and akin to not answering every call is us slowing down and taking a pause. It is a must. When we slow down it signals to ourselves and everyone else that everything is going to be all right. That the work is being done and has been done and we deserve a break. That this intentional slowdown or even pause is not a luxury for us Black women, it is a necessity. We need to make sure we build it into every aspect of our lives. As Black women, we have spent most if not all of our contribution to this world working, pushing, and hustling with little rest. Our rest has been already earned. Now is the time to take it.

The best real-world example I know that demonstrates how important pauses are is in the medical field. In surgery right before the surgical team is about to make an incision, they take what is called a time out. During the time out, they confirm things related to the patient and the surgery to ensure that everything will be done correctly. This pause ensures that things will go all right. A time out is something that can even be repeated multiple times during a surgery to ensure a better outcome. It doesn't require any additional resources. It doesn't cost or sacrifice anything to take one. We need to take time outs in our lives, Black women. Time outs in our lives also need to be taken with the confidence that they are important and they don't mean we are sacrificing our lives moving forward if we take one. We need these time outs to be able to not only rest but reflect on all things related to our lives. What better time to confirm the ideas, goals, and direction we want our lives to go in than a time out that we can repeat as many times as we want.

Earlier I talked about how being anxiously overwhelmed forced me into a time out and that when I came out of that feeling, things had continued on without me just fine. The same applies to you. When you take your time out so that you are giving yourself that time to evaluate and align your life—and hopefully in your case it is voluntary and not anxiety driven—know that everything will be all right and continue on. The world must get used to Black women intentionally not filling their time and leaving space for these essential pauses. Slowing down and pausing is our time out. And as much as we can use this time to reflect, we shouldn't be inclined to fill this downtime with more stuff to do. We can also just rest. I don't know about you but in the past, I have felt guilty resting and actually not doing anything. I'd always find ways to do things more often than not during my "rest." I've explored with my therapist why I felt guilty not filling every hour, including rest, with some sort of activity, even if it's mental work. For me it came down to wanting to control any outcome. I was not trusting that things will be OK if I'm not thinking about them all the time. How many of us Black women truly don't trust the outcome when we are resting? To truly be free to rest, we have to practice having nothing to do or plan or think about in some of our periods of reset. We have to trust that true rest that leads to better outcomes for ourselves involves periods of nothing, just us and our breath.

A habit I've incorporated into increasing my rest and trusting of the outcome is setting aside twenty minutes daily for just me and my breath. Sitting breathing and clearing my mind.

What also frees us from being overly concerned about the outcome is what we focus on. One thing I know is I no longer spend any significant time thinking about people or things that don't concern me. When I concern myself with my work and my rest, the outcome is a given. My husband likes to say "it takes the time it takes" any time I get frustrated about how something is progressing. He has an understanding that, if you are to go through a certain amount of seasons to get to a certain outcome, you will still have to go through those seasons. Imagine how much longer those seasons become and how much longer it takes you to reach your desired goal if you spend a significant amount of that time focused on other people and things outside of that. To be able to have the confidence that what is for you is for you because you think it, you work for it, and you believe it, means that your primary concern has to be you.

At this point in my life, I know that even what other people say about me can't concern me. I remind myself "So what?" just like my therapist says, when I get sidetracked with "he says" or "she says," any time I get distracted into being concerned. It's a bad use of our time and energy to be concerned about what other people say about us. It seeps into the time it will take us to get where we need to go. I can't think of how many times as a child my mom would say "Mind your books," a common Jamaican phrase that Jamaicans will tell you is a highlight of Jamaican parenting. But besides the obvious intention to make sure you know that their concern was for you to concentrate on your school work, it tells you as a school-age child that you should mind what is most important to you during that time of your life. Imagine how easy it becomes to focus on your own seasons in life when you mind whatever represents "your books" during that time. If you did that, how much confidence would you have that everything would work out or eventually be all right? I would have a lot. How could you not when your focus is refined and undistracted?

Black women, I want us to have the ultimate peace. That peace comes from knowing everything will be all right. When we trust who we are—hard-working, committed, and deserving women—we can be rest assured that what is for us is for us. Nothing can change that, not even our own rest.

Truth #12

Your Authentic Self
Is in a Silk Cap

The day after I went on the first date with my now husband, I sent him a text message with a picture of myself. It was a close-up of my face. No makeup, no recently flat ironed hair, barely awake. I took it staring into the camera on my phone, almost like a mugshot. I snapped the photo before I blinked again for the thousandth time. I added a note in the text message I sent along with the picture: "This is what I look like all the time."

And then I waited.

I was kind of nervous but at the same time I wasn't. I was nervous because the night before, I'd picked up what I thought were authentic vibes from him. It was a seven-hour date of just conversation and discussing life plans. We left nothing undisclosed, and it was the first time I'd been that vulnerable with someone. We told each other the ins and outs of who we were in a let's-get-this-out-of-the-way-now kind of way. I got home that night already having thoughts that he may be the one, and I felt comfortable thinking that.

Besides, we were equally yoked on all the Black Girl IRL points that mattered to me.

Me sending the picture was just another step in my mind of putting it all out on the table. If I was going to date this man, or even marry him, he had to know that last night's conversations were unfiltered, and how he saw me should be too. I didn't want to set the expectation that every day was going to be a glam day if he was going to be living a life with me. So I sent the picture, because I figured it could go one of three ways: he could not respond and ghost me, he could say something awful (I hoped he had more tact than that, but you never know these days), or he would appreciate it and respond in a way that reflected that.

He responded immediately, "I love it!" And I thought, *Yep, he's the one.*

I've come to really enjoy my authentic self, the one that takes absolutely no effort to be at all. It's what has made me more aware of the things that require my effort and are inauthentic to me. These things aren't always bad; they often stretch us and grow us in ways that we would not have done on our own. But, because I know who I am authentically, it has to be a conscious decision to do those things. I've spent a lot of time doing things and being things that were not me, and it is tiring. Try being an already exhausted Black woman, and then add in living a life inauthentically. It's a life of no rest.

My authentic self allows me to flourish in my comfort zone. Yes, the dreaded comfort zone. But being in a comfort zone isn't always a bad thing. I think of it like cruise control or autopilot. I know the destination and there's no question that I'm going to get there. But I'll get there with consistent effort over time. I can't take my hands off the wheel and expect everything to be fine. When you're in your comfort zone, it doesn't mean you're slowing down. You just know your speed and your capabilities.

In your comfort zone, you can navigate speed bumps, curves, you name it, because you know what you're doing. Both hands are on the wheel; you're not getting thrown off this road. When you dedicate time in your comfort zone, life goes well. So when do you come out of your comfort zone? When you need a new speed. When changes need to happen inside and/or out. When the old ways just aren't working and it's time to set a new pace to cruise at. You rev it up to get there and then you're back to pacing in authentic flow.

I rarely stay in overdrive; few things benefit from being in full throttle all the time, including me. But we have different gears for a reason.

Another plus of being in my comfort zone is that's where I tend to do well and so do my relationships with others. I'm not overly anxious, nervous, or doing things just to do things. In my comfort zone, I unlock the parts of me that truly are everyday Black girl magic: The part of me that checks in on the ones I care about most and remembers what matters to them is empathetic without constraints on my emotions. The part of me that shares my experiences, because I know it can be relatable to other Black women. My vulnerability opens the door to them to share who they are too. Or the part of me that wants to explore what is new and absorb it all at my own pace. It allows my creativity to flourish. Comfort has glorious effects on my life.

And as much as I enjoy getting dolled up—cute outfits, hair done, the whole nine—on some of my best days, I shamelessly embody what the comfort zone probably looks like. When people talk about being their most authentic self, I know what mine feels and looks like. It's in a silk cap, you hear me?

Silk cap, hair tucked in, socks and an oversized T-shirt (because I'm always cold), cup of coffee, and I'm so good.

If I'm not there literally, that's where I set my mind. As our authentic selves, cruising in comfort, we are able to power through the work we need to get done, come up with new ideas, and be the best friends, partners, moms that we can be. There's no comparisons or pretenses. We're dialed into who we are. We move through our purpose with our focus locked in.

Have you ever really thought about who you are when you let your guard down? When you say what you want, when you want? What your version of no-fuss, silk-cap-mode is? You are your authentic Black girls in real life when you are in whatever that is for you. I know it looks different for all of us, but I *know* you know that feeling when you feel empowered to show up as yourself, no matter what that looks like, and your confidence tells you "I got this."

No-fuss-silk-cap-mode is just so peaceful for me. I recently realized that although everything isn't the best it can be all the time, I feel the best I've ever felt despite challenges. After thirty-eight years, I feel like I've settled into myself fully and authentically. Like I've finally taken a seat in my life and have stopped running from one pretense to the next. And I do it without concern about what other people may think about it. I truly feel comfortable knowing that I'm not for everyone, and I actually don't want to be. My peace requires that type of resolution. If it requires seeking validation, then it's not for me.

Getting comfortable being comfortable with yourself is a daily effort and, if you're new to it, it takes some practice. I started off telling myself that this is who I am and it is what it is. Did I wholeheartedly believe that upfront? Of course not. Are there times when I still doubt this? Of course, but talking to ourselves and telling ourselves who we are is the first way to affirm that. After all, your own voice is the most important voice; it's the one you hear most often. Telling myself who I am doesn't mean I'm not evolving or trying new things, but it means I am led by my own voice, not by others.

Living an authentic life as the Black girl I am really is so fulfilling, and watching it in other Black women is equally as encouraging. More and more Black women are letting their guards down for themselves, the most important stakeholder in their lives. Have you ever had a face-to-face with your silk cap self? It took decades before I finally met her, and oh how I appreciate her. She really helped me lean into being myself. It wasn't easy but I had to tell myself to be me, first. Often the last conversation I was having was with myself. Do I like this? Do I want to do this? Does this resonate with the life I want to live? Too much is required of us, Black women, to not be prioritizing these types of conversations with ourselves.

It was the same thinking when I sent my now husband that deal-breaker photo. You're either going to take me as authentically as I am, or don't even worry about it, was my thinking. I knew I couldn't spend a lifetime being the show version of myself. That was the realization I got early on when I started reframing my dating process. As I'd said, I got comfortable with being with me, alone, and comfortable with what this me looked like. And when it came to future partners and people I invited in my space, you needed to be OK with that transparency as well. The transparency I am able to give myself is loving and kind, and it's the type that I know doesn't come easy for the world to give to me naturally, so I do it for myself. It gives me grace, whether I'm in the right or the wrong, and it makes sure I know I'm still loved. I knew I wasn't OK with letting someone else in if they didn't honor that as well.

You know what's the most transparent thing I've realized about myself? It's the biggest truth that emerged from every truth I went through. Being a Black girl in real life is amazing. It's not only amazing, but also empowering. It's every bit of flyness people on the outside may think it is and then some. I remind myself of this daily. Why? Because it's easy to be distracted from this reality.

When we are being pulled in so many directions and having to constantly provide input, it's easy to get exhausted holding this title. Yes, being a Black girl is a title. We can forget that every responsibility is not our responsibility, and not everyone is equally yoked for our attention and time. The title of Black girl is one we are born into, but it isn't given lightly. It comes from generations upon generations of other Black women who have awed with their everyday magic and upheld our significance.

Have you ever watched a Black woman singer or actress perform? It is always amazing. The amount of character and confidence they can put into a show gives me chills. To know that these Black women are also Black girls in real life isn't lost on me. I know that, just like us, on the other side of the performance, the expectations have always been higher and the effort has always had to be more. These women— stars to us—live with some of the same truths we do.

This book was about some of my Black girl truths, but not all of them. Some of the ones that I've lived through, learned from, grown from, and at times laughed from. Sharing these truths have helped me stay in my authentic self, to settle in and feel good about it. Why? Because I know they resonate with other Black girls too.

Some days it may seem like everyone is living like Beyoncé, the side of her that we see, that is, the perfect performance of a lifetime. Then I get knocked back into reality quickly. All it takes is one text from my friend that she's running late because her kid just had a meltdown or me being in my car signing a birthday card as I'm stuffing the envelope with a gift card outside the birthday dinner I'm about to walk into late. Because this is real Black girl life. This is the everyday stuff that we pull off and show up for while leading whole lives in every other area because it's expected of us. This is the everyday magic: a Black girl in real life, balancing life and all that it throws at us like no other.

And sometimes when this life feels out of balance, it takes just one gut check to know I've been doing and saying too much. I'm not the one who has to answer it all, and I definitely don't need to be the be-all and end-all for everything. Even more so, taking a step back is a way I protect my Black girl peace and harness my inner greatness so that everything keeps going. It doesn't make me oblivious to the world and what's going on. It just makes me mindful of what really matters to me and not waste too much time on anything else. Will people try to ruffle this Black girl's feathers? Yes, yes they will. Do I need to react every time? No, no I do not. Does that mean even the people closest to me may even push me to what feels like my limit? Of course. I know this and I have the tools to protect those relationships. It's not always about defending myself to no end.

To that end, when we think about relationships, Black women—the thing that so many of us want and can be such an important part of our lives—we absolutely must lean into who we are and what we want, especially from a life partner. We don't have to settle. Set your Black Girl IRL Partner Rating System in place with whatever set of criteria you've deemed as most important to you, and use it out in the dating world. Is the methodology foolproof? Probably not, but it certainly can cut out the noise and bring more people who reflect what is important to you into your life. It also holds you accountable and reaffirms the importance of being equally yoked. Remember we can't want in someone else what we don't have in ourselves. But all in all, let's own our process and get clear on everything so we are being prioritized like we deserve to be.

The truth is, Black women, that we are the ones that overdeliver on everything, relationships included. But what about the relationship with ourselves—are we overdelivering there consistently? We should, and we deserve to lean into those the most. To live as unapologetically as ourselves as we can. To keep what works for us and let go of what doesn't without fear of things not working out, because in the end, with drive like ours, it will always work out. We must set our sights on what we want and what is for us. We are limitless, so let me be clear, everything is for us. Let's make sure our relationship with ourselves reflects the love and care of someone who can take on these just about everything goals.

When I think about being a Black girl, I feel good. I feel privileged and you should too. Privileged to be part of a group of women who are resourceful and intuitive and have persevered through it all. There is so much that gives me chills about us. Who we are is much more than a look, it's a state of being. Whether we are glammed up or laid back, we are always a reflection of being on point.

Our ultimate truth is that wrapped up in all the truths is an authentically wonderful woman. A woman who deserves everything good that comes her way and knows how to weather the storm through anything that is not. We must make a habit of taking it all off—the pressure, the influence of others, the expectations—and sit with ourselves and let our guard down. And whether we're in our silk cap or not, that's our time.

Use that time, Black girls, to speak your truth to yourself so you can really believe it and affirm it. Then take that truth and go into the world and live it because, girl, we are needed. Black girls, in real life, with real lives, living our lives, we've long been the influence and magic of this world.